BELOVED LAND

STORIES, STRUGGLES, AND SECRETS FROM TIMOR-LESTE

GORDON PEAKE

SCRIBE
Melbourne • London

Scribe Publications Pty Ltd
18–20 Edward St, Brunswick, Victoria 3056, Australia
50A Kingsway Place, Sans Walk, London, EC1R 0LU, United Kingdom

First published by Scribe 2013

Map of Timor-Leste drawn by Nigel Peake
Typeset in 11.75/16.25 pt Adobe Caslon Pro by the publishers
Printed and bound in Australia by Griffin Press

The paper this book is printed on is certified against the Forest Stewardship Council® Standards. Griffin Press holds FSC chain of custody certification SGS-COC-005088. FSC promotes environmentally responsible, socially beneficial and economically viable management of the world's forests.

National Library of Australia
Cataloguing-in-Publication data

Peake, Gordon P. (Gordon Patrick), 1973- author.

Beloved Land: stories, struggles, and secrets from Timor-Leste / Gordon Peake.

9781922070685 (Australian paperback)
9781922247308 (UK paperback)
9781922072689 (e-book)

1. Nation-building–Timor-Leste. 2. Timor-Leste–Politics and government–2002-. 3. Timor-Leste–History–21st century.
4. Timor-Leste–Economic conditions. 5. Timor-Leste–Social conditions.

959.8704

This project has been assisted by the Australian Government through the Australia Council, its arts funding and advisory body.

scribepublications.com.au
scribepublications.co.uk

Scribe Publications
BELOVED LAND

Gordon Peake was born in Northern Ireland, and gained a Bachelor of Laws from Queen's University before attending the University of Oxford, where he acquired a Master of Philosophy in Modern Middle Eastern Studies, and a Doctor of Philosophy in Politics and International Relations. He has worked as a researcher and consultant in a number of countries in the developing world, and has published widely on peacekeeping and police reform.

Dr Peake has held positions at the University of Ulster, the International Peace Institute in New York, and Princeton University. He lived and worked in Dili in 2007–11, and is currently a visiting fellow at the State, Society and Governance in Melanesia Program at the Australian National University.

For Suzanne and Charlie, aka Murak

Contents

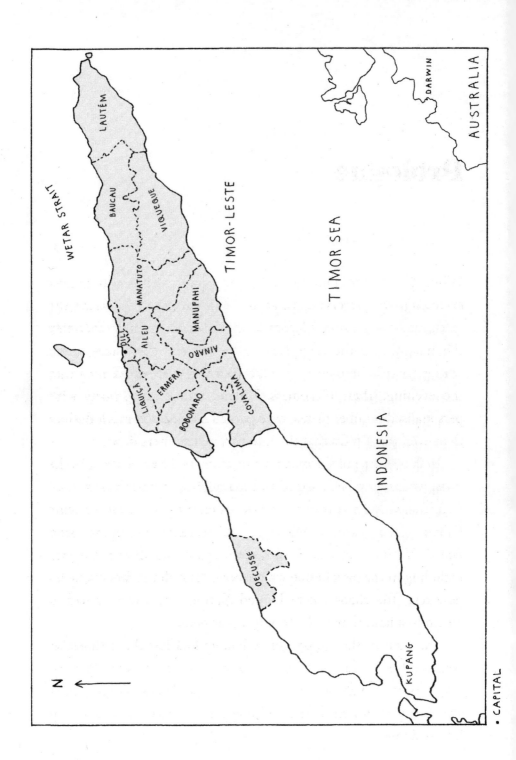

Prologue

When I came to Dili in 2007, the Hotel Timor was almost exclusively the preserve of what the Timorese called the *malae*, the foreigners. By the time I left four years later, it was most definitely the hangout of the new Timorese elite and their hangers-on who gathered there *en masse* each morning and stayed long into the evening. Their Hummers, Pajeros, and Prados, many with personalised number plates, were parked outside and much flashier than even the 4WDs that the international advisers drove.

In 2006, some of the men now smoking and chit-chatting in the hotel would have been armed and marauding around the streets of Dili. That was the year of the 'crisis', when the police and the army fell apart and nearly one-tenth of the country's entire population fled their homes in fear. Tented cities sprang up all over the city, including in the park beside which, nowadays, all the fancy vehicles now rest. The chaos meant United Nations peacekeepers had to return to a land they had left only a year before.

The men in the smoky coffee lounge had left those times far behind them. Materially, many seemed much better off, with whispers they were getting rich quickly, as heads of companies awarded government contracts to repair the roads and build up infrastructure.

A white, cavernous building erected during Indonesian times, the hotel would not have been out of place in a Graham Greene novel. I could never get enough of the place, and could while away hours there, watching people and catching up on the latest tittle-tattle and reading the daily newspapers that fascinated me, no matter how similar each day's stories seemed to be compared to the last. I'd come back home smelling of cigarettes and clutching arcane bits of detail and new pieces of personal connection.

Just before I left Dili, a friend from Israel came to visit and I took him down to the coffee shop, which, as per usual, was shrouded in cigarette smoke, intrigues, and dodgy deals. On that particular day, my friend was not the only visitor. Jose Manuel Ramos-Horta appeared in the lobby, surrounded by a small security detail. The former Nobel Peace Prize-winner also took up residence in the coffee bar, chatting away to a shapely middle-aged woman in blue who was clearly dressed to impress. No one else in the coffee shop paid the party any attention. Perhaps they could not see them through the thick fug of smoke.

'That is the president?' queried my friend. 'In Israel, they would clear an entire hotel for a leader to have a coffee. It's amazing to think that this guy was shot and nearly killed a few years back.' He was even more surprised when I told him that affiliates of the men who shot the president were sitting at a nearby table, wolfing down a club sandwich and playing on their iPhones. And that wasn't the strangest thing I saw in my time there — not by any stretch.

This is a book of travels, histories, and recollections about a country that, like my own, Northern Ireland, often only enters the world's consciousness when something goes wrong. But Timor-Leste is much more than a narrow narrative of conflict and violence. It is a story of the long shadows of Portuguese colonialism and the lasting impacts of Indonesian occupation. It is about reconciliation and the politics (and often business) of forgiving and forgetting both what the Timorese have done to each other and what their former recent occupier, Indonesia, has done to them. It is about developing a common tongue that all people in this territory can speak; Timor-Leste is home to one million people who speak nearly twenty different languages. Ever more, it is a story about oil and gas and the ability of the current crop of leaders to steward this resource for an expanding population and for the generations to come. It is about how difficult it is to establish a state from scratch in a country of finely threaded personal connections and colourful personalities where no bit of information stays secret for long.

Timor-Leste is also an international story, and its significance goes beyond this small territory just north of Australia. After looking away when it was strangled close to its birth in 1975, the international community helped deliver this state into the community of nations nearly a quarter of a century later. For three years, from 1999 to 2002, the United Nations ran the entire country, and donors have invested billions in it since, trying to accelerate the process of building a state that historians tell us takes centuries. Yet this massive outlay has done little to raise the majority of the population from deep poverty. It is relatively easy to identify where a lot of the money has been spent: it has gone into salaries for international staff, many of whom have difficulty communicating with the average Timorese. However, I did meet many qualified and capable expatriates who worked in Timor-Leste and who, in contrast to the overall direction of international aid efforts, did in fact play an important and integral role in building this new state. They came from different backgrounds and were involved in different areas of activity, but all of these effective workers shared one common trait: they had stayed for a long time and were not hopping from one part of the world to the other in search of the next unusual passport stamp.

For both Timorese and internationals, this is a story of intertwining personal histories, hope and despair, ambitions and frustrations, personal flaws and strengths, and, sometimes, tremendous hubris and naïveté. At its core, this book is a story about people. It is a story that shows how much the international community still has to learn if it is to help rather than hinder the nation-building process.

As this is a book of stories, let me begin by telling my own and how I ended up in what, for me, was the farthest corner of the globe and certainly a world away from the 'peace building think-tank' in New York where I'd been working the previous years — a place where the solutions to every complex problem seemed to be another report or another conference. The work was all slightly removed from reality: the dappled, messy, and all-too-human world in which decisions were made was under-acknowledged on paper, as was the capacity, intent, and abilities of individuals charged with implementing them. I was delighted to finish up.

A few months after I left its padded walls, I was asked by a university in the UK to conduct a study about what the fighters who had fought against the Indonesian occupation were doing now that independence had been won. How I was considered competent to do this was anyone's guess, but I had spent a week or so in the country in 2005 and at least knew my way from the airport to town.

I returned to a country that was very different from the one I visited, as the 'crisis' had occurred in the intervening year. What had begun as a labour dispute between disgruntled soldiers from the country's western districts had escalated into shootings between the police and the military, and within the police force; house burnings; a mass exodus of people from their homes into camps; the resignation of the prime minister; and the return of foreign troops and police less than a year after they had left. These events tarnished the former United Nation's poster child for successful peacekeeping.

The impact of the crisis could be most clearly seen from the air as our plane circled over Dili. What had been green spaces were now canopied with white tarpaulins — roofs for the tens of thousands of Timorese who had been displaced during the fighting. We flew directly above one large sprawling camp on our approach into Dili's President Nicolau Lobato airport, so named after a prominent Timorese political leader who had been killed by Indonesian troops in 1978. I had my passport marked with a satisfyingly large stamp, and as I sweltered in the humidity of the baggage hall, it suddenly hit me that I was meant to conduct a research project in a country about which I knew comparatively little (at best). I waited with some Jordanians who had also arrived as part of the United Nations Police Contingent. They were as much strangers in a strange land as I was, the difference being that they were meant to enforce a law that they probably had yet to read.

The taxi driver could only say two words in English — 'ten dollars' — but he did know the way to the hotel, and we drove in the sort of embarrassed silence that descends when two people can't speak to each other.

I was staying at the Hotel Dili near the waterfront, renting one of the six small rooms at the back and sharing a tiny bathroom with the other occupants. 'What are you doing staying here?' thundered a friend when he arrived and discovered that I didn't know some story about the hotel's past which, apparently, 'everyone knew'. I told him I didn't really have much of an option. At $35 a night, it was probably one of the cheapest rooms in a town dominated by expensive hotels. At least it was clean and quiet. At night I'd have drinks with some of the other guests, many of them working as 'advisers' in government departments but using English to address the waiters who served the beer. One guy was assisting the government on 'reforming the telecommunications system' and breaking the monopoly of the single 'phone provider', Timor Telecom. He didn't speak a single word of the Portuguese that the telecoms law was written in, but seemed unperturbed by this. He was staying in one of the nicer rooms, which was no wonder, as his salary details were leaked onto the Internet a few years later. He had been earning nearly US$600,000 a year, and had not needed to encumber the taxman with an income-tax return. By the time I left Timor in 2011, there was still a telecommunications' monopoly, until it was eventually ended in 2012, just before parliamentary elections. I also discovered that the pro-Indonesian militias had previously used the rooms as a staging post in 1999 and, earlier than that, Australian intelligence had used them while listening in to the sounds of the Indonesian invasion. The past was everywhere.

My work got off to a bad start as Julio Tomas Pinto, the Timorese researcher I was meant to be working with, announced that he'd been offered another job. 'I'm sorry, *malae*,' he said, 'but I've just been asked to be Secretary of State for Defence — but don't worry, I can help you with your research project on the weekends.' He'd gone from earning less than a hundred dollars a day with me to ministerial office. I told him he'd probably have his hands too full to be transcribing interviews for me and he said that, on balance, I was probably right. He found me someone else to help me finish it. The project was professionally fulfilling but personally heart-breaking. Its goal was to find out what had happened to many of the former fighters demobilised after the conflict, and the answer needed not the lengthy report I produced but two words:

'not much'. Hour after hour, day after day, I listened as my new research assistant translated their tales of despair. 'All we got is a medal,' they would say. How were they meant to feed their families with a medal? It was all the more upsetting because these old men thought that I could do something about it, and that my research project would conclude in something beyond mere words that were unlikely to be read in detail — much less acted upon.

For want of very much else to do, I ended up staying in Dili months longer than was probably necessary to finish the study. I began to learn a little of the Tetun language, a mixture of Portuguese words layered onto a more local structure. I liked going for walks back and forth to Christo Rei, the large statue of Christ the King, at the far end of town — a gift to the Timorese by Suharto, the Indonesian dictator, whose forces invaded Timor-Leste in 1975. I also discovered that my coming from Northern Ireland had surprising cachet. Thousands of Timorese had crossed the seas to my homeland to work in chicken factories, and the Timorese I talked to spoke about *Irlanda Norte* with something approaching reverence. I'd never heard my country described in such glowing terms before.

I ended up staying much longer than I originally intended. I was offered a job with an Australian-funded policing program, and I was so pleased with my fancy title of 'Senior Policy Adviser' that it took me two weeks to realise that I didn't have the first clue what I was expected to do. Eventually, I went to work in the Office of the Secretary of State-Security, Francisco da Costa Guterres, who was Julio's counterpart for the police. I still remember the first day I went up there, I knocked on a door marked 'The Office of Conflict Prevention and Security Management' and found that there was just one person behind it. Three years later, it was he who suggested a name for my son.

I loved almost every day I was there, especially when it involved taking meandering journeys all over Dili and throughout Timor-Leste — a place where one person's story leads to another that intersects with another, which, over time, opens up a little more of the bigger picture of how and why Timor-Leste is the way it is and how it is developing as a country.

I sat in dilapidated, old government buildings with broken windows and clogged toilets, and listened to old veterans, who had fought against the Indonesians in the forest, rail angrily about having been left behind. I went inside sacred houses where the spirits of the Timorese ancestors rested, and saw a faded Portuguese flag taken delicately from a wooden box with a reverence similar to that given to the Turin shroud. I drank warm beer with ex-rebels while their children stacked plastic glasses outside in the dirt. I clambered around overgrown forts and became claustrophobic in a bat-infested cave where the fighters had once lived. I heard stories about how some of these men had returned from the dead, and how others could make themselves invisible through believing in a magic stone.

I rarely tired of trying to sort fact from fiction in Dili, a city where sometimes the main activities of many seemed to be the creation of intrigue and the mongering of rumour. I lost more money at cockfights than I probably should have done. I filled so many notebooks with the circular complaints of international advisers that I thought I could write a tragic-comic novel. I heard tales of financial chicanery that made me want to cry, but as many stories of bravery, courage, and decency that made me feel ashamed to live in such a nice house in Dili.

I crossed the border to West Timor to talk with ex-militia leaders charged with the most horrendous of crimes but who claimed that the families of their victims had forgiven them. To hear other stories, I had to go back home to Northern Ireland and spend time with the thousands of Timorese who live and work there, not far from where I was born. At every turn, I met heroes and villains in a land where everyday lives are grounded in custom, connection, and resistance.

People often ask me why I ended up spending over four years in a place in which it was my original intention to spend four weeks. There are many reasons. A major one is that I found great personal happiness there. I met the woman who would become my wife; for that, I will forever be grateful. In part, it was because I got to see — from the inside — how the peace industry works and doesn't work, and to watch as a new country was built up before my eyes. The experience confirmed that peacekeeping and development certainly had very little to do with the dull and wordy tomes produced in the air-conditioned rooms of a think tank. But perhaps another reason was also because I felt strangely at home in Timor-Leste almost from the first day I arrived. In many ways it reminded me of a hot and humid version of where I was brought up.

Timor-Leste's connections, relations, arguments, and loyalties, and its divisions that had become histories recounted and retold into what is held to be truth, reminded me of my own divided island. Both countries often seemed entirely made up of historical backstories. In neither place could the reach of the past or the capacity, intent, and abilities of individuals be separated from what was going on in the here-and-now. Both are places where government policy was trusted or distrusted, depending upon the person who had launched it rather than what was actually in it, which often had very little to do with formal policy pronouncements. Even though I had travelled far, I felt that I had never left home. The Timorese call their country *rai doben*, which translates into English as 'beloved land'. After living there for four years, I pretty much felt that way about it, too.

Chapter One
The Portuguese Monument

I parked my car near the trees and walked down to the small weather-worn monument that overlooked the beach. Two cannons sat in front of a small tower with the Portuguese coat-of-arms stuck on the top. The inscription reads, 'Here marks the disembarkation of the Portuguese on 29 August 1515', and on the stone base of the column are the words, 'This too is Portugal.' Five hundred years ago, this shoreline would have been one of the southernmost places in the discovered world.

This is Lifau in Oecusse district, the enclave of Timor-Leste that is hemmed in on all sides by Indonesia, and a place where, because of local beliefs, the fish in the sea are still not caught or eaten, although many people go hungry. It is a quiet, untended place that feels a world away from the clogged bustle of Dili, which is a nausea-inducing, ten-hour ferry ride away. I've been to the Lifau monument many times over the years but never met any other visitors. But it is central to my story, and it is where the story of Timor-Leste begins.

No one knows for sure the names of those Portuguese who made landfall on the foreshore that day, but their intentions were probably not as transformative as the foreigners who now live in Oecusse, most of whom work for the United Nations or various aid organisations. The newcomers then were probably traders in search of profits from forests rich in sandalwood and bees. The timber's sweet scent made it good for paring down and burning as incense, and the beeswax was used to make church candles. In the sixteenth century, these goods were among the most lucrative commodities in the world. Timorese sandalwood on a Brahmin funeral pyre in India was a marker that the deceased was a man of especially high standing.

Accounts of this history aren't to be found in Oecusse. Beyond the inscription on the monument, there is very little in the way of written history about the centuries of Portuguese rule that began in Lifau to be found in this dry, mountainous place or even in the rest of the country, for that matter. There is no national library, and I could find no articles or books of relevance in the campus of the main university in Dili. There, the stacks were sparsely filled with musty and dog-eared Indonesian textbooks. A man with a clove cigarette dangling from his mouth, who I think was the librarian, looked at me blankly when I asked if the university had any sources that related to the last five hundred-or-so years of Timor-Leste's past. To find out the story, I had to go elsewhere.

Bizarrely, one of the largest single repositories of dedicated material on Timor-Leste in the southern hemisphere is to be found inside a walk-up tenement block in the city of Darwin, in northern Australia, in an apartment where the curtains never open in case sunlight should yellow the precious contents that are inside. Apart from a small camp bed and a photocopier that takes up most of the bedroom and a small kitchen, the remainder of the apartment is like a mausoleum dedicated to the island that is located an hour's flight away. The collection is all the more extraordinary for the incongruity of its location.

The apartment belongs to a monkish former shop-clerk called

Kevin Sherlock, who appears to have taken it upon himself to gather every conceivable piece of material on Timor and arrange it to fit neatly into every cranny of his living space. The books on his shelf are like a timeline of Timorese history. They recount the eventual end of the Portuguese colony in 1975, the Timorese civil war that followed, and the nine-day republic of late 1975 that was declared but snuffed out by the invading Indonesian army. He had books about the 'Balibo Five', the Australian and New Zealand newsmen murdered in cold blood by the advancing Indonesian army, and the cover-up on the part of the Australian and Indonesian governments that followed. The books were written by Jill Jolliffe, a doyenne of Timor correspondents, a close friend of Kevin's and a woman who, like him, had dedicated most of her adult life to working on Timor. Other books emphasised the country's bloodstained recent past. Titles such as *A Dirty Little War: an eyewitness account of East Timor's descent into hell* and *If You Leave Us Here, We Will Die* may sound like garish potboilers, yet they are anything but that: they are sober and well-researched accounts of the Indonesian invasion and the gory end to that occupation, when mass violence followed a poll in 1999 wherein the majority of Timorese voted for independence.

On a crowded desk waiting to be allocated a space were books, edited volumes, reports, and conference proceedings about the first ten years of the country once it was restored to the community of nations. This material chronicled a story not too dissimilar to that told about many countries that became independent after a long postwar liberation. Following three years of United Nations administration, the books dealt with how the Democratic Republic of Timor-Leste became independent once again in a midnight ceremony on 20 May 2002. Following high hopes, things took a dip downwards during the 2006 crisis when the army and police fought pitched battles in the streets of the capital, security collapsed, and

United Nations peacekeepers were required to return just as they were about to declare 'Mission accomplished'. Perhaps the only book that was absent from this collection was a 'Sex and the City in the Tropics' style romp about the antics of randy (and oft-times inebriated) peacekeepers during the United Nations administration of 1999–2002, which was as different from the dry bureaucratic reports churned out by the United Nations as is possible to imagine.

Kevin's compilation of contemporary material was impressive, but was only a small fraction of the entire library. The biggest part of his collection related to the centuries of Portuguese rule. The little apartment was filled with shelves and shelves of archival material about Timor that have been neatly photocopied over many years from public records' collections in Lisbon and Macau, and arranged in vellum folders in year-by-year order from the seventeenth century onwards.

Now in his late seventies, Kevin's collecting mania began after a short holiday visit to the then territory of Portuguese Timor in 1974. He appeared to have been bitten with an even more acute case of 'beloved land-itis' than I suffered. After that, this shy, courtly man taught himself Portuguese in order to plumb the archival depths of a colonial administration renowned for keeping detailed lists and exacting records about even the most trivial detail. By way of example, one of Kevin's files was a scintillating account of the metallurgic qualities of each medal given out to the Timorese kings by a visiting dignitary from Lisbon. His attention to arcane detail comfortably matched that of even the most punctilious Portuguese pen pusher. He has also clipped out the newspaper wedding announcements of Darwinians who, in the 1950s and 1960s, honeymooned in Timor. It was to Kevin's house that I went to find some archival material about the arrival of the Portuguese on Lifau.

I hadn't intended to stay for too long with Kevin — an hour at most. Friends who had called on him recently had reported he was in poor health, having suffered multiple small strokes and illnesses over the last few years. He certainly did not look well: stooped and sallow, he had the appearance of a man who rarely saw the sun. But my visit seemed to energise his frail frame. When I told him I was interested in learning more about the early settlers, and about the style of book I was interested in writing, he scooted around the apartment with his walker, tracing his fingers over the box-files, and selecting sheets of paper that he thought would suit my purpose, collecting up the material and then photocopying it for me. Although he'd never been to Oecusse he seemed to know almost every detail about the place and every article that had been written about it. At one point, I was starting to flag and said that I hoped I wasn't tiring him out. 'I live for days like this,' he said and kept on searching.

I read how the inscription on the monument might trick a visiting sightseer into thinking that a permanent Portuguese settlement was established in 1515, but this was not so. As with much about Timor-Leste, what is publicly presented isn't necessarily the full story. Merchants, explorers, and Dominican friars did stop by every now and then, but, generally speaking, Portuguese interest in the island was pretty slight for many years; their attentions were fixed on trading posts in Africa and elsewhere in Asia. The island was run by an endlessly changing alliance of local kings known as *liurai* and colourful swashbuckling opportunists known as *topasses*, in whom Portuguese 'sovereignty' was vested. Their name derived either from an Indian word for 'interpreter' or a Malay word meaning 'top hat'.

No one knows where the *topasses* came from, but it was certainly not Portugal; some historians trace their origins to dalliances between the Dominicans and local women on nearby islands. The two most prominent *topasses* families were the da Costas and the Hornai, reputedly the descendants of a renegade Dutch buccaneer. For nearly two centuries, these families alternated between collaborating with and conspiring against each other to exploit the forests for trees and beeswax. The men married multiple times, each union creating a new political relationship and replacing a previous alliance. Eternal vows of fealty could sometimes last little more than a few months. The more I read the bewildering narratives of conciliation, rivalry, inter-marriage, forgiveness, strong-arming, secret understandings, and ever-shifting affinities during the 1600s and 1700s, the more I felt the cadence of politics in present-day Timor-Leste.

The *topasses* donated money to Lisbon in return for being left alone. For nearly two centuries this arrangement suited everyone. Problems started when Portuguese interest in the island they dubbed the 'Isle of Sandalwood' increased after the Dutch booted them from their prized possessions in Asia in the late-17th century. With fewer and fewer remnants of their empire left, Portuguese attention turned to their territory on the eastern edges of the mapped world. The first governor to Timor was appointed in 1702; upon his arrival in Lifau, he might well have surmised that previous postings in Angola and Mozambique were tame by comparison. He immediately found himself at the centre of a violent feud with his supposed allies. Although respectful of the crown, the da Costas — at that point the dominant bosses — were less than captivated by the prospect of being knocked off the top perch or sharing the profits of their business ventures.

Despite having 'loyal' subjects like the *topasses*, the Portuguese quickly found themselves under siege in their little stockade. The new governor prevented outright defeat by hiring soldiers from local *liurai* in return for dishing out privileges, such as baptismal rites and the conferment of grandiose titles — a tactic that his successors would employ for many years to come, and a strategy not dissimilar to that adopted now by the Timorese elite. Although these ploys bought time, granting vassalage to one family and not another, they also served to exacerbate petty frictions and rivalries — another consistent feature of Timorese politics to this day.

Overgrown ruins of one of the Portuguese forts reputedly built at the time still stand and overlook Pante Macassar, the main town in Oecusse. Off-duty international staff often walk up there to work up some sweat in the afternoons, and local people visit to lay flowers at the well-tended grotto to the Virgin Mary that is just inside the crumbling walls. On the way up, an inscription in Portuguese and the local language of Baikeno peeks out from the undergrowth. The plaque reads, 'Lifau was conquered with the cross of Christ, water and salt and not with arms.' The inscriber was being a bit heavy on his or her magical realism and somewhat economical with the truth, because for months at a time the Portuguese barely ventured forward from the increasingly fetid fort. Life there sounded truly god-awful. Food was scarce, with dogs, worms, and grubs eaten as staples in order to survive. Relations with the *topasses* waxed and waned; skirmishes between those in the fort and those outside were regular occurrences. I read how, twenty years after the arrival of the Portuguese, when the da Costas were loyal and the Hornai families weren't, the Portuguese faced a new assault, led by warriors spiritually fortified after swigging on a mix of palm alcohol, transfused blood, and the indeterminate fluids of a black-and-white dog. It was one long melodrama of rain, hunger, exhaustion, and betrayal. It was no wonder that they decided to move on.

In 1769, the Portuguese cut their losses in Lifau and moved further eastwards and to a quiet bay on which they founded a new capital, Dili. The location afforded enhanced security, protection, and a calmer place for boats to moor and, crucially, fewer *topasses* around to rain trouble down upon them. The da Costas and Hornai families shifted their attention to frustrating the efforts of the Dutch on the western side of the island. The Portuguese kept Oecusse for nostalgic reasons, but didn't do very much with it.

Not that there was that much more dynamism in the new city of Dili, either. The colonists did not advance much beyond it for the next one hundred and fifty years as they ran their possession on a shoestring and battled disease, the glare of the sun, heat, boredom, and themselves. The outpost was so poor that the Portuguese governor even had to rely on the beneficence of his fierce rivals, the Dutch, for sea passage in and out. The colony was desperately poor. Most money in the state coffers came either from 'contributions' demanded from Chinese businessmen or from selling territory to the Dutch.

Visitors to Dili vied for the most unflattering description of this remote corner of the Portuguese Empire. The botanist Alfred Wallace visited in 1861, and each page of his account feels steeped in stagnancy and colonial neglect. Dili was a 'most miserable place' where at any one time half the population seemed to be down with malaria. Not a single mile of road had been built beyond the capital in over one hundred years. Another man well qualified to opine on stagnant European settlements in the tropics was Joseph Conrad. He described Dili as 'highly pestilent', a place where the chief occupation of the colonial officials was to accuse hapless visitors of bureaucratic transgressions and then demand a high price to 'resolve' the problems they themselves had created.

In stark contrast to their present-day successors in international organisations who try to conceal their frustrations in the ever-rosy progress reports, the Portuguese officials seemed congenitally incapable of spin when they reported on their work. Every opportunity to vent was availed upon with alacrity. Many of the diaries and official reports of Portuguese who were based in Dili during the eighteenth and nineteenth centuries are misery memoirs of resentment and petty jealousy. Far away from home, they filled page after page with lamentations at the failings of others, coupled with accounts of incompetence at all levels of the administration. 'Even a fertile imagination could not conceive of the depths of our misery and abandonment,' groaned one melancholy civil servant in the 1850s. Poor quality of staff was a persistent complaint. As the English did with Australia, the Portuguese used the settlement as a dumping ground for political agitators and criminals that they wanted to get rid of, hence making governing progressively more and more difficult. By all accounts, the territory's 'administration' appeared to consist of too many incompetent, self-aggrandising ne'er-do-wells, and too few with any semblance of managerial or organisational skill. This is how the governor summed up the problems in a despairing letter to his superiors in Macau in 1879: 'I have a total of forty-eight Civil and Military officers, of which ten are competent, ten are mediocre and seventeen are useless ... the Judge Delegate tells me that he knows nothing of his duties.' Ineptitude, lack of interest, and internal bureaucratic battling began long before the current crop of international visitors to Timor. Another consistent thread across the ages was that the trouble being complained about was everyone's fault but that of the person who was doing the complaining.

The linguistic divide between the Portuguese newcomers and the Timorese was rarely bridged. Very few Portuguese learned any of the native languages and dialects. Perhaps for that reason they seemed to spend very little, if any, time with the native Timorese, who are mentioned strikingly few times in their diaries and reports.

When they do get a look-in, it is often in pejorative terms.

Although the Portuguese claimed the eastern half of the island, along with Oecusse, and divided it into separate kingdoms, this declaration reflected their aspirations on a map rather than the facts on the ground. Even in the latter half of the nineteenth century, fewer than one hundred colonists lived beyond the city, and large parts of the island were uncharted. For centuries, no one seemed particularly certain even of where the island ended. It was not until the 1920s, when an expedition reached the eastern tip of the island, that the matter was settled.

In the late-19th century, the Portuguese turned to the *liurai* as they sought to expand their reach beyond Dili. The rationale for getting beyond the city was both financial and political. The bottom had fallen out of the sandalwood market many years previously, and the colony was flat broke. The Portuguese administration in Macau, which was responsible for Timor, made it clear to successive governors that no money would be forthcoming. Equal to the number of doctors it had, Portuguese Timor had just one customs officer, with the net effect that the state was only able to collect extremely minimal amounts of tax revenue. There was also a very real political imperative. Although the Portuguese had claimed the eastern half of the island as their own, they needed to demonstrate their presence beyond Dili in order to stave off any territorial claims from the Dutch.

The Portuguese pinned their hopes on a small bean that had served the Dutch so well: coffee. The colonists handed large numbers of beans to *liurai*, who were then asked to plant them and bring a percentage of the profits back to them in Dili. In return, the kings would receive an honorary title, a flag, and an elaborately calligraphic certificate: the Portuguese simply did not have any money to pay them.

Coffee cultivation was a sound idea. Timor's damp mountain soils were ideal planting grounds and, initially, all seemed to be going well. The beans sprouted and production was high. The problem was revenue collection. In the absence of enforcement, many *liurai* decided to sell the coffee beans and to pocket the profits. To claw back the money, the Portuguese hired the warriors of a nearby *liurai* as tax collectors. This itself proved hardly a fail-safe strategy as, on many occasions, the *liurai* who were sent out to get the money hoodwinked the Portuguese and also kept the stash. The tribute received from coffee was rarely enough to cover the outlay of hiring warriors to go off and get it. An added disadvantage was that it exacerbated divisions between nearby areas, and often ended bloodily. The taking of skulls was a regular feature of tribal wars. In accord with most things in the country, the scalping of heads would also follow a strict ritual and was an activity carried out in deference to hierarchy. Ricardo Roque, an anthropologist whose book on headhunting in Portuguese Timor is replete with many pictures of severed heads, writes about how heads were cleaned, the brains taken out and, thereafter, smoked so as to ensure that they didn't go mouldy. In battle, some warriors would carry the heads of previous conquests around their belts. Some skulls were commandeered by the authorities and shipped off to museums in Macau and Coimbra in Portugal. The revenue-raising experiment was an unqualified disaster.

Parallel efforts on the part of the Portuguese to create their own coffee plantations also ran asunder. Many growers lacked both the practical knowledge of how to grow coffee and any interest in acquiring the knowledge. 'What we need is an Agricultural Department made of people not only familiar with coffee cultivation but also with the island and its languages,' moaned the governor in 1893, echoing the sort of conversations heard among frustrated international staff in Timor one hundred and ten years later. The preference of many for supping coffee in Dili over heading out into the districts is also little changed. (I once knew someone who proudly told me that he'd never been out of Dili in the two years that he was in the country, and that this was unlikely to change unless a four-star resort was built. With supreme irony, his last portfolio was 'district development'.)

The Portuguese administration decided they needed to collect revenue in another way, but their replacement tax proved extremely onerous and, for them, dangerous. They decreed that they would impose a 'head-tax' on each Timorese male over the age of sixteen and impose levies on everything from rice to fruit trees. Few people anywhere like the idea of tax, but this was especially the case in a place in which the colonists had done so spectacularly little for the natives. The *liurai* were especially furious, as the Portuguese cut them out of the collection system, undermining their authority and depriving them of valuable opportunities for graft and pocket-stuffing. Many had sworn undying fealty to the Portuguese, but these oaths mattered little now. Spontaneous revolts broke out in and around Dili, Oecusse, large swathes of the east, and on the frontier line between Dutch and Portuguese territory.

The most famous of these revolts began in and around the town of Same in Manufahi, a region that begins amidst steep mountains and slopes downward towards the sea. The insurrection was led by a *liurai* called Dom Boaventura, whose name still holds currency today as the leader of Timor's first national revolt. A man of large girth, a photograph of him in warrior regalia and replete with huge sword and spear is iconic in present-day Timor. It is the Timorese equivalent of the Che Guevara photograph, and can be seen on T-shirts, stickers, mini-buses, and street art. The Nobel Peace Prize-winner and former president, Jose Ramos-Horta, claims him as a blood relative, happy to be associated with someone who gave the colonists a good poke in the eye. Boaventura has a community radio station named after him; he even has his own Facebook fan page. The Indonesian army erected a statue of him in Dili, apparently without irony. When I told some of my Timorese friends that my wife was pregnant with our first child, one from Manufahi said that, 'You could do a lot worse than calling him Boaventura.' (However, we settled eventually on Murak, the Tetun word for something that is priceless or a treasure, as his second name.)

What has been remembered burnishes the myth of the warrior, but eclipses the family rivalry and the intrigues and rumours that are equally central to Boaventura's story. He was, to some extent, an unlikely rebel leader, almost forced into his actions by blundering and insensitive administrative decisions. As revolts were breaking out elsewhere, his initial inclination was to seek some form of conciliation with the Portuguese administrator, but he was waved away and then slapped with a higher tax burden. If the high-handed official thought that this was the end of the matter, he was mistaken. The government horseman carrying news to Dili about how the impertinent upstart had been sent packing never made his final destination. The rider was hauled off his steed and killed, marking the first stage in the rebellion. Boaventura managed to unite and mobilise a coalition of *liurai* — most of whom he was in some way related to through marriage — to great effect. His warrior band followed up this first attack in spectacular fashion. They threw out the Portuguese from the central districts and threatened to march on Dili. The Portuguese military commander of Manufahi was murdered, allegedly at the hand of Boaventura's brother, Dom Vicente. With each victory, more *liurai* who had been unsure of whom to support joined the rebels' ranks.

The situation was sufficiently serious that a governor's letter to Macau actually received a response. Troops from Goa and Portugal's African colonies marched off the gunship *Patria* to join with warriors from other *liurai* who either simply didn't like Boaventura or were paid to side against him. The forces advanced from Dili up the steep hills towards Manufahi, surrounding each village on the way and offering a stark choice to the *liurai* in the area: surrender and send men to join with government forces, or have the village pummelled by artillery and grenades. Government forces burned the crops of everyone associated with Boaventura. Previously loyal supporters of the Portuguese who had become avowed followers of Boaventura changed sides once more. The national hero was becoming undone as much by machinations within his close associates as by his opposition's military prowess. The Portuguese didn't seem particularly perturbed by who joined their alliance, even welcoming Dom Vicente, Boaventura's brother, who was apparently so put out that his sibling took some of his cattle without permission; as a result, he turned against him.

The end was bloody. Boaventura and his forces found themselves encircled high up in the mountains and cut off from food and water, with their positions pounded by the *Patria*, which had steamed from Dili to the southern sea. Boaventura went out in a blaze of glory. He mounted his horse and charged down the mountain, his followers streaming after him. Miraculously, the Dom somehow escaped, but many of his followers were not so lucky. Thousands were executed, a process that took two days and nights. The Portuguese let their Timorese troops scalp the heads of their victims and take their trophies home with them.

The conclusion to the story is unclear. Some say that, abandoned by his own, Boaventura eventually surrendered to the Portuguese in Dili in 1913, a broken man, but there are no Portuguese records of this. For colonists who kept meticulous records of everything from the number of medals coined every year to the manifests of sailing ships in Dili harbour, not to have kept the proceedings from a famous trial seems peculiar. In their absence, myths developed about where the Dom had gone. I once heard he was killed and cut up, and that his bones lobbed into the cement mix that made the walls surrounding Santa Cruz, the largest cemetery in Dili.

The Portuguese crushed the *liurai* and took over greater administrative control of Timor, but then did practically nothing with it. Although the population were taxed, they received few services in return. There were just one thousand primary school students in the entire country in 1940. There was no electricity and no paved roads in Dili, and conditions out in the districts beyond Dili were little different from what they had been at the beginning of the century, or the century before that. This thin glaze of administration and modernity meant that anthropologists naturally gravitated to Timor because the social systems they were observing were preserved in aspic. Life continued as it always had done for the multiple groups on the island, which were divided from each other by different languages and dialects, and by the topography.

Among the first to chronicle life beyond Dili was the British naturalist Henry Forbes, who visited in the 1880s. He estimated that there were about forty different groups within a territory half the size of Tasmania. Difficult terrain kept many groups entirely separate from one another, despite the relatively close geographical proximity. Sharp, bony mountains rose up from the sea on both sides of the island, and rivers were difficult to ford for parts of the year and divided deep valleys from each other. Portuguese Timor was a mosaic of small kingdoms. Each group was organised along rigid hierarchical lines and ruled by kingly families of the *liurai*. The majority lived off subsistence agriculture, with small amounts of tithes (such as chickens) being collected by warrior clans to enable a *liurai* elite to live in modest luxury by the local standards of the time.

These groups kept no written records, but have long, detailed oral traditions about their beliefs and customs, which have been preserved by designated members of the community known as 'keepers of the word'. These practices passed from generation to generation, but they have only recently been documented either by Portuguese administrators or anthropologists.

Their accounts revealed a complex picture of social systems grounded in ritual and myths where almost everything — the sun, the moon, mountains, rivers and springs, rocks, trees, grass, animals, and foodstuffs — had been imbued with spiritual significance. Shepard Forman, an anthropologist, and his young family lived in the lands of the Makassae in the eastern part of the island in the 1970s, and he describes a social system where rice and pork, for instance, were metaphorically synonymous with sperm, and morning dew was the water that gave life to the land.

Each hamlet had its own sacred tree and sacred house in which hallowed objects such as spears, silver discs, loincloths, and drums, along with Portuguese symbols such as flags and insignia, were stored. I once visited a spirit house in which an ancient frayed parchment written in Portuguese was taken out with great delicacy from a rusted strongbox. Much of the writing had faded, and all that was detectable on the document was an embossed seal that was the colour of burgundy. The old man who opened the strongbox in which it rested asked me if I could hear the spirits whistling around the room.

The longer I spent in Timor-Leste the more I realised that the past had every bit as much pull on the lives of many as any formal law or edict issued by today's government in Dili. Some articles of faith had parallels in Catholicism, the dominant religion brought over originally by the Portuguese, but many of the beliefs and customs had their origins in practices that were in place long before the arrival of missionaries. Today, many people in Oecusse still have regular communications with their ancestors. I remember one senior civil servant telling me that their forefathers' views on matters often take precedence over those of official superiors. Timorese believe that the spirits of the dead can surely impact — positively or negatively — on the living world, depending on whether their edicts are followed or ignored. For that reason, trees and lakes in certain parts of the country are avoided, and there are prohibitions on certain foodstuffs. The family name determines which foods they may or may not eat. Some don't eat eggs, chicken, or coconut, and so strong is the adherence to these taboos that most Oecusse people maintain a prohibition on eating fish, even though it is among the most plentiful food in a district with a variable food-supply. Long before the Portuguese arrived, people believe that warriors from Oecusse made a bargain with a monster that helped them across a swollen river. That creature — a freshwater fish with the horns of a bull — helped them return safely to their lands, but only after extracting a promise that neither the men nor their descendants would eat food that came from the river or the sea.

I heard of everything from severe itching to calamitous injury being visited upon those who broke the promise. 'Can you believe that people eat fish from a can — I'd rather starve!' said one rake-thin Timorese to me one day. In other places, anything from hacking coughs and fevers to sterile unions, sickness, and death were thought to be the ill-effects of transgressing these spiritual prohibitions and upsetting the dead. The role of the supernatural is important. I came into the office one day and read in the paper that a member of the defence forces had, seemingly unprovoked, whacked an old neighbour to death with a shovel. 'She was a witch,' my colleagues said matter-of-factly, as if no more explanation was needed.

As soon as I felt I had begun to understand the codes and customs, I would learn more stories and find myself entangled once again. This interplay between ancestors, land arrangements, prohibitions, ritual, and superstition was often veiled, and seemed to change according to unseen rules to which I was not privy. The complex rituals and codes were hard for outsiders to understand, especially if they were only there for a short time and couldn't interact with locals in order to find out more. No wonder, perhaps, that so many international civil servants found it much easier to retreat back to the coffee shop or the pool table, baffled by the place to which they had been assigned.

No less important than the past are family connections. The anthropologists' descriptions gleaned from years spent in remote villages revealed the strength of a communal identity. Individuals were not islands but linked socially, economically, and politically through marriage and familial bonds. Godchildren, cousins, or people in the traditional structure were considered immediate family. Families were part of wider alliances forged through marriage. Timorese homes were places in which a 'nuclear family' lived with grandparents, cousins, uncles, aunts, and relatives connected through marriage. Matrilineal and patrilineal lines sat atop and across each other, creating an in-built social-security system in a land that had no effective government or official social-welfare mechanism. The net effect was that many people in the country seemed to have some form of kin relationship, in some way, to one another. No matter how well I knew the Tetun words for members of the family, I would never fail to find some of these connections bewildering. 'I know Lere very well,' a friend told me one day, talking about the craggy head of the Timorese defence forces, a man who once memorably claimed that there was nothing that any foreigner had ever done in history which impressed him. 'We are family. He's my husband's sister's mother-in-law's uncle,' said my friend. Being Irish, I probably have a similarly tangential connection to someone in Dublin or Boston, but I definitely don't know their name or phone number.

Ironically, although Portugal may have disregarded or even neglected its former colony, its influence endures and its imprint is more obvious in contemporary Timor-Leste than is the case, for instance, of the Dutch on the western, now Indonesian, side of the island. An early 1940s assessment of both sides of the island concluded that the Dutch had superior programs in such areas as bridge and road construction and education; but, today, apart from the graveyards of dead soldiers, a visitor would barely know that they had ever been there.

One of the most noticeable Portuguese legacies is in people's names. Timorese children are baptised with Portuguese names, and continue with the tradition of having two given names and two surnames. To be considered legitimate, the names need to be found in a thick church-approved book. A rollcall at a school in Dili would sound exactly like that of a school in Lisbon, or Maputo, for that matter. Often, but not always, names correspond to particular regions of the country, which means that they map where people come from and from which language group they originate. People with the surname dos Santos are almost always from the district of Liquica, just west of Dili; and the Babo name is synonymous with the hill district of Ermera, where the coffee is most plentiful.

Although the most obvious Portuguese legacy is Christianity, the religion did not in fact become dominant until Indonesian times, when identification with the Church became a way of associating against Indonesian rule. Even so, the religion practised now has a definite Latin quality about it. Grottos with white-faced saints are dotted around the country, and candles are lit as forms of remembrance. A representative of the Church opens most ceremonies. As in Ireland and other countries with large Catholic populations, there seems to be a saint for every occasion or profession. St Anthony of Padua is the patron saint of the Timorese police, and a statue of the balding monk in his coarse, brown robes is to be found outside each station and post. 'His hair would fall out completely if he knew what was going on inside that station,' an officer said to me one day, before revealing a complex tale of financial chicanery about which he'd been sworn to secrecy.

Even with Tetun as the *lingua franca*, the language of church documentation remains Portuguese. I married my wife in Dili, and our elaborately baroque wedding certificate is in that language, complete with a seal that looks like it had been moulded centuries before. Portuguese was thinly used as a spoken language during colonial times: only the *liurai* and elite families learned it in order to be able to communicate effectively and to curry favour with the rulers in Dili. However, many of its words seemed to percolate much more widely. Some researchers estimate that as much as half the Tetun words are derivates of Portuguese. Timor-Leste has a civil law system that is based to a large degree on the system used in Portugal and many of its former colonies. The law is written in Portuguese, despite the fact that only a small minority comprehend the language. Sometimes the similarities with Portuguese law can be too unerring, and suggest an extensive use of the cut-and-paste function on the part of languorous advisers hired to write the country's laws. For many years, the Timorese traffic code seemed as if it were an inverse of what it should be, and applicable to a country that drove on the right, not the left. The plan was an almost word-for-word reproduction of the Portuguese traffic code.

Another legacy hit me halfway through the second hour of a noonday repast in Lisbon a few years back: both these countries enjoy really long lunch breaks. A short one lasts about ninety minutes; an average one seems to last a good hour longer. 'Make it two-thirty' is often the response if the question is, 'Can we meet at two o'clock?' Perhaps as a consequence of the long break at lunchtime, the workforce has difficulty motivating itself once it is back at work. Timorese bureaucracy can be very slow and officious, with its officials being sticklers for the use of arcane rules and stamps. I once needed to obtain a certificate of 'good comportment' from the Ministry of Justice in order to be able to apply for an Australian visa. Getting my hands on this document required wading through layers of officialdom and visiting multiple officials, each of whom seemed to be located in a different part of town and with different opening hours (which didn't necessarily guarantee that the required individual would be in the office). When I eventually managed to secure all the signatures, I proudly went to the ministry, only to be told that I needed to present the documents in a red folder. 'If I get one now, can I come back?' I asked of the aptly named *funcionario*. 'No; you must return in five days' time,' he snapped, and shut the screen door. No wonder that red folders in the stationery shops were sold at a premium price as compared to other colours. A good friend says she carries a spectrum of coloured folders in her handbag so as to head off further delays.

The Timorese love titles and appellations, a double-your-money combination of Portuguese and indigenous senses of hierarchy. Almost everyone in the workplace seems to have a grandiloquent (Portuguese) title, no matter how understated or mundane their job would seem to be. I once visited a six-person police post in a deep valley in central Timor-Leste in which each and every one of the officers was a chief of something or another. One grizzled old policeman proudly told me that he was the 'Chief of Fuel', pointing to his place on the neatly drawn organisational chart that was prominently displayed on the wall. So what does that mean, I asked?

'I distribute the fuel vouchers and I fill up the tanks with petrol once a week,' he said proudly, becoming first baffled and then irritated when I asked him how he filled the other thirty-nine hours and forty minutes of his working week. Officers with equally ostentatious titles sat on dilapidated old chairs at other tumbledown posts throughout the country. An hour out from Dili, I met a Chief of the Armoury in Ermera district. His sole duty seemed to be to have the key to the door when the gun-safe needed to be opened. On the days he wasn't there, there was no access to the room. Government ceremonies, too, incorporate a large element of Portugal in them; two countries that love formality combine to produce doubly long events. The police and military parades go on for hours in the baking morning heat while the VIPs sit under the shade on leather couches, and the less fortunate invitees fidget and wilt on uncomfortable plastic chairs behind them. On one occasion, an unfortunate standard-bearer accidentally dropped the national flag during a ceremony. Newspapers led on the story for weeks, with headlines such as 'City of Dili Is Terrified', quoting senior politicians about the ill omens that this signalled. The last time the flag was dropped presaged the Indonesian invasion, the deputy prime minister declared. It was a reminder of what a place of superstition it is, as I was to find out when I went to meet one of the leaders of that dark period.

Chapter Two

The Testaments of Rogerio Lobato

There was no in-flight personal entertainment system on the Air Timor flight from Singapore to Dili. Instead, small TV screens attached to the ceiling of the plane showed a seemingly endless loop of *Funniest Home Videos*. The late-middle-aged man in the aisle seat opposite me was creasing up at the silent footage of skateboarding antics going wrong, and of the family cat picking at a bauble and setting in train a process that would bring down the Christmas tree and short-circuit the lights. He was munching on a packet of peanuts, and looked a picture of contentment.

The chortling man was Rogerio Tiago de Fatima Lobato, who, along with his colleagues, must go down as one of the most short-lived holders of government office in history. He was Minister for Defence of the Democratic Republic of Timor-Leste that was proclaimed on 28 November 1975 after the Portuguese pullout and snuffed out nine days later by the invading Indonesian army. But, unlike many of his colleagues, he had another chance. When independence was restored in 2002, Rogerio became minister of the interior, his term coming to an end when he was jailed for illegally distributing weapons during the 2006 crisis that had brought the country to its knees. Released early from prison on the grounds that he needed to seek urgent medical attention overseas, he left the country on a Lear jet lent to him by the government of Kuwait. The president subsequently pardoned him, and he was now a free man engaged, I had been told, in lucrative business activities. He was apparently an influential middleman between the Timorese government and Chinese contractors building the nation's electricity grid, and he had many and varied business interests in companies throughout the region. He had ingratiated himself with old party colleagues, and would karaoke with them at party gatherings.

This former teacher, soldier, smuggler, convict, entrepreneur, and minister looked the picture of health now, *en route* back from a medical check-up in Singapore that had been paid for, I was later told, by the government that had replaced him following the 2006 crisis. I never found out if this was true; perhaps it was just another Dili rumour.

I'd met Rogerio once, in 2005, when I'd led a study trip to Dili. I remembered that he seemed to have many mobile phones, and that the exclusive task of one of his many bodyguards seemed to be to hold them. He was charming and gracious, spoke impeccable English, and, as we left, presented each of us with a small wooden carving as a memento of our meeting. It was illegal to export sandalwood products, and I asked him what type of tree the keepsake came from. He gave me a conspiratorial wink and said, 'I am the law.'

Our plane touched down at Dili's President Nicolau Lobato International Airport, named after Rogerio's dead brother, who had been one of the greatest heroes of the resistance against Indonesia. We were all ready to disembark, but the flight attendants made us wait for the business-class passengers to exit first. Among them were three men in late middle-age who were greeted on the ground with much aplomb by a large welcoming party that included the minister of justice.

Rogerio also had people waiting for him when we eventually walked off the plane. He received a clenched-fist salute from one of the ground crew, and he handed his small carry-on bag to a guard from the Department of Building Security who was in uniform but not at work. Rogerio and his aide headed straight for the VIP lounge.

I saw a picture of the distinguished business-class visitors in the newspaper a few days later. They were senior officials in Portugal's Audit Court that monitored the execution of the state budget, and they were visiting Dili to discuss the possibility of setting up a similar institution in the former colony. The head of the delegation declared that, 'an audit court should become an instrument for transparency and accountability'. His words sounded scripted from an ancient bureaucratic ritual that he probably felt obliged to intone in order to justify the trip. The Timorese justice minister was quoted approvingly, saying that the visit was extremely worthwhile. It was the sort of endorsement any good bureaucrat would seize upon in order to write up the trip as a success. The minister's name was Lucia Lobato — Rogerio's niece. One of her first actions in office was to manage her uncle's release from prison. Practically her last task in office would be to plead that the prime minister should spare her from jail on charges of corruption.

For the thousands of international visitors with aid budgets to expend who have passed through Dili's airport over the last decade, places like Timor-Leste are like a blank canvas on which to paint their dreams. Their engagement begins when the plane touches down on the tarmac; for many, Timor-Leste is just like the *terra nullius* that the Portuguese thought it was when they came ashore nearly five hundred years ago. All too few see that the picture is already finely hued. You can see it in the VIP lounge, where many of the 'old generation' of leaders from 1975 and the 'new generation', who earned their legitimacy as activists agitating against Indonesia, come to meet their colleagues, friends, and family members off the plane. Many are greyer, and some are paunchier than they were years before, but their relationships with each other cannot be ignored. In this small place, personal relations have more implications for the politics of the present than any institutional innovation or grand development scheme.

Visitors from Lisbon and many other places see Timor-Leste as a nation state with institutions, agencies, committees, policies, and procedures. They do not see it as a tangle of family relationships, friendships, romances, and antagonisms that collectively render ideas and concepts such as 'accountability' and 'separation of powers' almost completely impractical. The state is not anonymous: the small and tightly bound elite may have institutional titles, but it is hard to separate their office from their own personal relations and long histories with each other. Who you are, where you come from, who your relations are, and your links and associations are more important than anything else in this small island nation. Kinship and opaque connections are the ties that bind — not five-year plans and detailed strategic documentation. Everyone knows everyone, or something about everyone. International state-builders either cannot see this, or choose not to look.

About a year after I saw him on the plane, Rogerio decided to run for the presidency — a position that didn't have as much power as the prime minister, but was nonetheless one of considerable influence. I rang one of his fixers and arranged a meeting with him at his campaign headquarters, which, as it turned out, was directly opposite a massage parlour.

The candidate was running late because of the heavy traffic, and

I killed time in the waiting room where, the day before, he had launched his campaign. On the wall behind the table where he had held his press conference someone had glued two small wooden crocodiles and a wicker basket that said 'Dili, City of Peace'. To the side were an expensive-looking electric keyboard and some speakers: the candidate had apparently belted out some tunes to enliven the launch. An old woman dressed in black was sweeping the same stretch of floor back and forth with such dead-eyed intensity that I thought that it might cave in under her.

I stood up to examine his election poster that looked like it was dipped in sepia. The most prominent image was that of the sixty-something candidate himself, wearing a sharp, dark suit and a look of steely determination. By his side was Nicolau. One of his staff saw me staring at the poster. 'His brother is supporting him,' he said, 'even from the grave.' It seemed death had not parted them. 'Success in human endeavour,' he said, 'depends as much on the dead as the living.' This distilled in a single sentence some of the wider findings of many anthropologists who have lived and studied in Timor-Leste. Respecting, remembering, and listening to deceased ancestors are the keys to granting everything to the living, from succour and protection to fertility.

My ruminations about how ghosts interplayed with the present in this deeply spiritual and supernatural place were interrupted by the noise of a car roaring into the driveway. Everyone suddenly appeared busy. This could only mean one thing: the candidate had arrived. The cheery man who bounded into the room about five seconds later was much thinner than when I had first met him, and was filled with spry energy. He wore a yellow golfing shirt and an expensive-looking pair of slacks, and his brown slip-on shoes had dainty tassels. He ushered me into his reception room and we sat down on the slightly musty, high-backed felt chairs while a helper fetched some coffee. He padded beads of sweat from his forehead with a handkerchief. There was something terribly old-fashioned about his demeanour. His affectations were a solicitous throwback to a bygone age.

He started talking before I'd managed to fish a pen out of my pocket. The first thing he wanted to do was quash the argument levelled by some that this run for presidency was a vanity campaign. He claimed to be confident about his chances ('What would be the point of running otherwise?'), and he recited a raft of campaign promises. As president, Lobato would make his first priority reanimating discussions between his country and the oil companies that had been deadlocked for years over the question of whether gas should be piped to the southern coast of Timor-Leste or Darwin. He would strive to create a better business environment for small Timorese enterprises and foreign investors alike. He would strengthen Dili's already good ties with Beijing, but would not consider the establishment of a Chinese military base on Timorese soil. His satisfyingly expansive campaign themes were 'unity, solidarity and strength'. He hadn't got around to preparing a written manifesto.

But, mostly, he wanted to talk about the past. We were meant to speak for thirty minutes, but our meeting ran nearly all morning. He handed his four phones — some things never change — to a minion, and started to tell me about his dark, rip-roaring adventure story of a life. He deserves a book of his own, rather than a chapter whose primary purpose is to lay out the importance of blood and belonging in a small place.

Rogerio was born in the late 1940s into a *liurai* family in the cloud-covered hills near Bazartete just outside Dili. The Portuguese had given his grandfather coffee beans to plant during their ill-fated attempts to make the territory turn a profit, and the town in which he was born is still ringed with coffee trees.

His childhood was hermetically sealed from the outside world. While other countries in Asia were already either independent or racked by anti-colonial insurgencies, isolated Portuguese Timor was seemingly immune to the political tumult elsewhere. Most of the population could not read, and foreign news was strictly censored. Young Rogerio thought that Indonesia extended only as far as the city of Kupang in West Timor and had no idea it reached across a vast archipelago of over a thousand islands. Gruff and distrustful colonial bureaucrats rarely granted visas to journalists, but those who somehow sneaked in wrote about a torpid land where time seemed to stand still. Australian journalist Osmar White visited Timor in the early 1960s; he was looking for adventure, but found instead tropical lethargy and foreigners who had fallen to melancholy in the unrelenting heat. White wrote that the island had 'the air of shabby frustration which broods over all places inhabited by generation after generation of subservient and unhappy people.' Even in the late 1960s, this was still a place where Portuguese officers expected the Timorese to stop and salute, or bow before them, when they passed by.

With journalists excluded, the little self-enclosed island seemed of interest only to anthropologists, hippies looking for one last exotic adventure before heading back home, and intrepid sightseers from Darwin. Needless to say, back in Darwin, Kevin Sherlock had faithfully clipped newspaper accounts of their recollections. Two teenage girls who went in 1965 reported that they'd seen a 'native funeral, a barbaric cockfight, wonderful native dancing and some incredibly old people', voting the trip 'a fascinating experience'. Many of the Australian visitors were newlyweds. In the 1960s and early 1970s, Portuguese Timor was marketed to Darwin lovebirds as a honeymoon destination in the same way that Bali is nowadays.

After leaving school, Rogerio joined the Portuguese army and rose to the rank of lieutenant, making him one of the few Timorese to achieve officer rank. In his spare time, he worked as a Latin teacher; one of his students remembered how the class conjugated with relish the words *amare* and *matere*, to love and to kill, every lesson. He chose texts about the Roman wars for students to read for homework, and told his classes that the Timorese should act as if they were centurions, prepared to defend their land from barbarians over the border. The reality may have been much less cinematic. One journalist (accompanied by his minder) who visited the frontier in the late 1960s used less elegiac words to describe it. 'Half-a-dozen Timorese soldiers drifted about and a dog lay somnolently in the dust,' he wrote. As well as Latin, all told, Rogerio speaks at least five languages. An Australian friend of mine who worked in his office remembers how Rogerio used to correct his English on draft correspondence.

In the mid-1970s the pace of events in Portuguese Timor quickened from sleepy to high-speed within the space of about a year. In a place renowned for near-total inactivity, an entire political trajectory seemed to happen at once. Rapid decolonisation was followed soon after by the formation of political parties, a brutish civil war, a declaration of independence, and, finally, an Indonesian invasion that gobbled up a state that was just nine days old.

The train of events began in 1974 with the 'carnation revolution' in the Portuguese capital, Lisbon, which swept away sixty years of right-wing dictatorship and, with it, the provinces of the Portuguese empire. The army that led the overthrow was fed up with being shot at in wars that seemed to have no end in Angola, Guinea-Bissau, and Mozambique; they couldn't wait to get rid of their possessions in Africa, and didn't see much reason for keeping their toe-hold in Asia, either. A new governor was dispatched to Dili with unsentimental instructions to get rid of Portuguese Timor as quickly as possible, no matter how. The Portuguese troops began to grow their hair long, and many stopped showing up for work.

The Timorese were divided as to what would be the best option for the future. Newly formed parties had a wide range of views, and had armed affiliates to aggressively press their points home. One party wanted to create a monarchy; others sought autonomy within a Portugal that no longer wanted it; some wanted independence; and others still wanted a linkage with Indonesia, which coveted the territory. Violent rhetoric quickly turned into violent acts that reflected local score-settling and the re-ignition of older grievances more than abstract debates on political status. In the first years after independence, the Timorese Truth and Reconciliation Commission has recorded a catalogue of ferocious beatings, beheadings, disembowelments, and executions that villager wrought onto villager during the civil war. The Portuguese army did little to subdue the fighting; many of its Timorese troops chose to take sides rather than keep the adversaries apart. Sensing the game was up, the governor fled Dili for the island of Atauro, taking with him two platoons of parachutists and fifteen thousand bottles of beer. Rogerio told me that the fleeing colonists dumped thousands of their weapons in the sea on the way so they could not be used.

Rogerio and Nicolau were leading members in the party that was victorious in the civil war. The party was called FRETILIN (Revolutionary Front for an Independent Timor-Leste), and styled its name, manner, and fiery rhetoric on the leftist guerrilla movements in Portuguese Africa. Its leading lights were all in their mid-twenties, and many of them are still central figures in Timorese politics, forty years later. Mari Alkatiri, a member of the island's very small Yemeni community, was a member of the party's central committee and would become the first prime minister following the restoration of independence in 2002. Another leading light, then and now, was Jose Ramos-Horta, the son of a deported political agitator, who would go on to to share the Nobel Peace Prize and be a future president. Ramos-Horta himself had been deported already. He was exiled to Portuguese Africa for, according to one story, writing a review of the Australian movie *Ned Kelly* in which he lauded the roguish Irish brigand as a role model for all peoples under a colonial yoke. Rogerio was renowned as the most aggressive of all the young hotheads, although there were probably a few other candidates for this 'accolade'. When a visiting newsman dared to question the truth of one of Rogerio's statements, the young revolutionary planted a gun against his head.

With little preparation, the brothers Lobato were flung onto the world stage. Their first overseas visit was to Africa to confer with their fellow revolutionaries in Mozambique who had also recently shaken off the Portuguese. On the way to Maputo, they stopped in Perth and at the homes of oil executives. Australian companies had been searching for oil in the Timor Sea, and the brothers went to stake their claim on behalf of a new Timorese government. They arrived at the meetings wearing combat-stained shorts and T-shirts, and flopped onto the floor. The movement's 'elder statesman', a customs official at the ripe old age of thirty-seven, called Francisco Xavier Amaral, and, reputedly, a descendent of Dom Boaventura, accompanied them.

FRETILIN's victory would prove pyrrhic. Indonesia was making ever more frequent encroachments over the largely undefended border, and there were no centurions to halt their progress. Five Australian and New Zealand journalists who chased the rumours of an invasion to the border town of Balibo found that their citizenship made no difference to the incoming Indonesian soldiers and their Timorese partisans. The newsmen were killed in cold blood.

The revolutionaries hoped that a unilateral declaration of independence would stop the Indonesians and, in a hastily arranged ceremony in Dili on 28 November, the party proclaimed the Democratic Republic of Timor-Leste. Originally, they had intended 1 December as Declaration Day, the same day that Portugal restored its independence after Spanish occupation. The decision to bring the date forward was made so quickly that Ramos-Horta, who was visiting Darwin, did not even know about it.

In a solemn ceremony outside the government palace that took place at the height of a stiflingly hot day, the Portuguese flag was lowered, and a red, black, and yellow flag with a white star rose in its place, which closely imitated the flag of FRETILIN. The new country's flag had been designed the previous evening, and a seamstress had been up all night stitching it together. The black triangle inside the flag represented the obscurantism that the revolutionaries believed that the rulers of the new state would need to overcome. A young cameraman called Jose Alexandre Gusmao filmed the ceremony, but subsequently lost the footage in the chaos that followed. He would later be much better known by his nickname, Xanana, and would become perhaps the most recognisable personification of the Timorese resistance.

Xavier Amaral proclaimed the new republic, and Rogerio read out the constitution, a one-page document that had also been prepared the night before. Rogerio wore a Portuguese army dress uniform that he had found inside the wardrobe of an office in the government palace; a captain had left it behind when the colonial administration had fled so hastily to Atauro. The other leaders were all dressed in military fatigues, and gave clenched-fist salutes to the camera — the same sort of signal I had seen used to greet Rogerio with on the tarmac when he got off the plane.

FRETILIN had the enthusiasm, but neither the personnel nor the experience to run a country of their own. There was not one doctor or one engineer in the entire country. The single economist in Timor-Leste was immediately drafted in as minister of the economy. Emblematic of how the civil war had divided families, this new minister's father was a leading supporter of integration with Indonesia. At the time that his son was taking the oath of office, the father was, along with Indonesian troops, preparing himself at a staging post in West Timor for the invasion of Timor-Leste.

Looking back on his youth, Rogerio said that they were too hasty in declaring independence, and maybe long-term autonomy would have been a better staging ground for the economy. 'But we were young and full of ideals,' he said, sipping his coffee. 'We didn't know just how difficult a situation we were in.' In 1975, Rogerio was just twenty-six years old.

Nine days after the national flag was raised, and with the tacit consent of Australia and the United States, who feared that a FRETILIN-run Timor-Leste would become a communist outpost in the South Pacific, and who thought the place would be unable to govern itself, Indonesia invaded and duly annexed the territory. The American president, Gerald Ford, had given a nod and a wink to the invasion during his visit to Jakarta a few days earlier. Australian intelligence officers also had their ears glued to the goings-on, and the Australian government did nothing — an original sin that the Timorese refuse to let their southern neighbours forget. An Australian hotelier named Frank Favaro was apparently earning extra money as an intelligence agent, and let out one of the waterfront rooms in his establishment for a large listening device. The hotel still has the same name — Hotel Dili — where I stayed when I first moved to Timor. Favaro's son is a Dili-based businessman.

Rogerio was sent abroad a few days before the Indonesian invasion — in order, he said, to 'draw the attention of the world to our cause'. He got out just in time, as he would surely have been killed if he had stayed. He lost his wife, parents, and each of his twelve siblings during the conflict. Nicolau left Dili and led the Timorese from the hills until he was ambushed a few years later; his head was taken away as a trophy for the Indonesian president. Nicolau's wife died a vicious death on invasion day, one of her last acts being to hand over her young son to a relative for safe-keeping.

The Indonesians had a policy of seeking out and eliminating all members of the Lobato family; the graves of many are still unmarked, and Nicolau's bones have still not been returned to his family. As a young adolescent, Lucia, the future minister of justice, hid in the forest to avoid being captured after an Indonesian dawn raid. She heard her mother cry out that the Indonesians were gone, but Lucia thought that there was something odd about the tone of her voice. She peeked out and, seeing an Indonesian gun pointed to her mother's head, stayed where she was, not uttering a sound until, some hours later, she heard an Indonesian helicopter take off. Her mother and six of her siblings had been rounded up and taken away. Lucia never saw them again.

Rogerio spent nearly a quarter of a century trotting the globe in exile, a sort of revolutionary Forrest Gump. He was received warmly in Pol Pot's Kampuchea and, in return for their hospitality, spoke at public meetings in Lisbon and elsewhere about how the Khmer Rouge was simply misunderstood. The Chinese and Vietnamese governments and Western Saharan rebels gave him military training before he eventually headed to Mozambique, where he tried to procure weaponry.

He took his short fuse with him. At one point in the late 1970s, he held a number of his Timorese comrades against their will, apparently for over a month. The Timorese exiles were living in a compound down near the border with South Africa, when simmering tensions over money and status turned violent. Among those held hostage were his colleague in the central committee, Mari Alkatiri, school friend Ramos-Horta, and Horta's pregnant wife, Anna Pessoa Pinto. Later, he was arrested for smuggling diamonds in Angola and sentenced by the country's Politburo to prison, where his time there was no doubt enlivened by weekly lessons in Marxist dialectic from another Timorese friend, Roque Rodrigues. I heard whispers that his former colleagues had tipped off the authorities in Luanda about Rogerio's extracurricular business activities. I was told that he bargained his way out of jail in exchange for providing information on human-rights abuses in Angolan jails; the Timorese he entrusted with smuggling out his correspondence was apparently the person Rogerio suspected of having betrayed him in the beginning.

The comings and goings of the small Timorese elite is reminiscent of a plot to one of the dizzyingly confusing low-budget soap operas from Brazil that are shown on Timorese TV most nights. The same characters are in all the episodes, and they connive, conspire, and intrigue against each other one week, making up with each other the next. Ever-lasting alliances are proclaimed and then torn apart in an endless search for power and status. Occasionally, the characters do completely inexplicable things that you would think would permanently estrange them from the group, but which only seem to make them more resilient. No one ever gets written out of the plot for too long, and continuity of position is not particularly important. It's all eminently watchable; perhaps because it is hard to predict what will happen next.

Returning to Dili in 2000, a quarter of a century after he left, Rogerio said his first task was to find his mother's bones. They knew that she had perished on Mount Maubere in the central part of Timor, and, soon after he arrived, he made a pilgrimage up its steep banks. He travelled with his cousins and traversed the rocky scrabble, calling out her name in Portuguese, Tetun, and their mother tongue, Mambai, hoping that their footfalls would awaken her spirit. After days, they thought it was all in vain and despondently trudged back down the mountain. On the way, they noticed some goats rubbing their bodies against a tree as if they had lice that they wanted to smooth out of their skin. They were utterly dejected and paid little attention, but the goats made so much noise that Rogerio said it sounded almost as if the animals were somehow trying to communicate with them. The men turned around, by which time the goats were bleating and using their hooves to dig out the ground under the tree. 'We found my mother's remains there,' he said, 'and I made a promise to her lying there below me that I would never do wrong to those who had done this to her, nor ever forget them.' I wondered what the development imaginers sitting in air-conditioned cubicles elsewhere in Dili would have made of a story about telepathic goats. They probably wouldn't have ranked it as being terribly important, or might even have thought it laughable; a distraction in the way of the real business of discussing matrixes, planning frameworks, and their own articles of faith.

While we were talking, a nervous-looking assistant, with a phone in his outstretched hand, knocked and silently mouthed that someone important was on the line. Rogerio waved him away with an imperious flick of the hand. He still had more stories to tell. He wanted to tell me about his tenure as a minister, a term that ended in ignominy in 2006 when he was jailed for dishing out weapons to a shady militia group. I was glad I had brought an extra notepad, as

I had filled one already. Rogerio was just getting started.

He fast-forwarded to 2002 when, after three years of United Nations administration, he became minister of the interior in what was called the Second Constitutional Government. (The First Constitutional Government was the nine-day administration of late 1975.) There was something of a concertina-like quality to this new government. Many of the faces that smiled from the picture after they had taken the oath of office in 2002 were the same as those who briefly occupied ministerial positions in 1975. Mari Alkatiri became prime minister, and Jose Ramos-Horta was foreign minister. Horta's now ex-wife revolved in and out of a number of the offices of the new state. Anna Pessoa Pinto was the first justice minister, then a member of parliament, and she is now prosecutor-general, somehow fitting in time in all this to design the uniforms for some units of the Timorese police. Not surprisingly, Rogerio Lobato and Anna Pessoa, the woman he purportedly held hostage, apparently cannot be in the same room as each other.

As minister of the interior, Rogerio Lobato ran his portfolio in the same way he'd seen government offices being run as private businesses in former Portuguese colonies in Africa. One of his first appointments was a former business partner from Maputo. The Mozambican's salary was apparently paid for by the United Nations Development Program (UNDP) on the un-ironic grounds that the tropical gangster in question had demonstrated expertise in 'financial management'. He hired a miscellaneous crew of associates, friends, and family members on state contracts. Few had the experience to administer very much, perhaps explaining why so many had ill-defined roles.

Rogerio's ministry sounds like a cross between a baronial court and Tony Soprano's back office. A visitor recalls a senior police officer leaving Rogerio's office with a crumpled uniform and looking extremely shaken up; as he entered, the minister who was constitutionally charged with civilian oversight of the police was returning a Glock pistol to the shelf. 'He wouldn't listen to what I wanted him to do,' Rogerio apparently explained. A friend and colleague who worked with him said the only time that Rogerio showed fear was when a passionate advocate for gender-sensitive community policing had tried to visit the minister. He had hidden under his well-appointed mahogany desk until the coast was clear.

Perhaps the major problem was that Rogerio, like many of his colleagues, wasn't terribly aware of how to undertake the job he had been given. He adapted quickly to fully funded foreign visits. He beamed with pride when the Australian prime minister at the time, John Howard, acknowledged him in the visitors' gallery on the floor of the parliament in Canberra. He loved the trappings of power and status.

But in a country with barely any legislation or procedures and few experienced personnel to allow ministries to function, he did not know what a minister was meant to do. In a land of training and workshops, he received none and, instead, construed his job to be some sort of unofficial head of the police, with responsibilities for wading into the minutiae of every issue, paying little heed to constitutional niceties. Secrecy, clandestine structures, connections, and distrust were the keys to the successful fight for independence, but not necessarily the attributes most useful to building an accountable system of government following the end to occupation. The new state remained a place where informal networks and relationships were often much stronger and more effective than a formal chain of command or legally prescribed duties.

A few years after Rogerio left the office of the interior minister, I worked in the same building, and was surprised that the people who worked with him didn't subscribe to the sense that he was a cartoon thug. They had seen men do much worse. Some remembered that he could be capable, on occasion, of incredible kindness. He was generous, and organised birthday parties for his staff; some explain his erratic behaviour as an understandable — if not condonable — consequence of a life punctuated by personal tragedies. In 2006, I was told, he gave his DNA to forensic specialists from the Australian police in order to discover if a headless body dug out close to where Nicolau disappeared was that of the dead leader. His hopes were raised, only to be dashed. The police told him that the body they had in the morgue was too degraded to extract DNA from. They would keep his sample on record and try again at a future point, when advancements in the technology might possibly enable another attempt. When the police left, the minister closed his office door and wept.

I had expected him to be sheepish about his role in the 2006 crisis, but not a bit of it. He was unapologetic about his involvement in distributing weapons, and claims his motives were misunderstood. 'Don't forget that I am actually the only one of the big fish to have stood trial and that I went to jail,' he said. Even his foes in Dili would concede that he had a point. A United Nations investigation recommended further inquiries into what senior figures in the political elite had or had not done during the crisis, but the Timorese leadership has not pursued these cases. 'There is too much political interference in the judicial system, which is why I am making justice a central campaign theme,' he declared, instantly adding another manifesto promise.

Younger members of the elite have just as deep and intertwined a set of connections. As Rogerio was rotting in an Angolan jail with only tomes on dialectical materialism for company, his niece, Lucia, was winning a scholarship to study law at university in the Indonesian port city of Surabaya. She became a member of an underground group of Timorese students who publicly agitated for the restoration of Timorese independence but also, more surreptitiously, helped to organise the transfer of supplies and information back to the resistance fighters who were struggling in the forest. They would meet in their university dorms, secretively swapping letters and communications that would go back and forth from Bali, Jakarta, and Surabaya to occupied Timor-Leste. She worked closely with her husband, Americo, and with a Timorese studying Indonesian literature called Fernando de Araujo (whose nickname was 'La Sama', meaning 'cannot be crushed') and a wispy-bodied law student called Longuinhos Monteiro. Longuinhos was serving as a member of the university honour guard, whose proximity and closeness to the Indonesians made him a valuable resource. He was able to covertly arrange the supply of uniforms and supplies to the Timorese fighters high up in the mountains. Although from a subsequent generation to Rogerio and company, their lives, too, are held in the same web of tight family connections, distrust, occupation, trauma, and short-term alliances that it is possible to read about but so hard to comprehend.

This new set of leaders has also waltzed in and out of the revolving doors of state. Lucia became minister of justice. 'La Sama' is a party leader, was the parliamentary speaker in the last administration, and is now the vice prime minister. A now much chunkier Longuinhos was the prosecutor-general, head of the Dili branch of Interpol, and is now head of the Timorese police; he used to go shooting on the weekends with Rogerio Lobato and another man, Alfredo Reinado, whom we shall meet in the next chapter. As police chief, he would fulminate regularly about the need for tough action against the country's martial-arts groups, but how much of that was serious and how much was bombastic rhetoric is a matter for debate.

Lucia's husband grew equally stout, and became a fuel-importing businessman. He was the first person I saw in Dili who drove a Hummer. His car had tinted windows, and its English-mustard colour had weathered rapidly in the sun. They lived in a house overlooking the sea, and apparently hosted all-night poker parties.

With such tight connections, the intended meaning of many of the concepts in the international donor toolkit, such as an audit court, can be difficult to comprehend, and no less difficult to administer. Although these individuals had formal positions, with clear constitutional distinctions between them, it was hard to separate titles and office from personal relationships, friendships, fall-outs, and long histories. These men and women played together as children and now see each other at weddings, funerals, and the multiple opening and closing ceremonies that accompany almost all endeavours. The elite know, or think they know, nearly everything about each other. In a way, they are family, and all families work to a logic that often makes very little sense to outsiders. Perhaps for that reason no Timorese politician seems to remain a black sheep in perpetuity, and the only way to understand how ministers behave is through using a family tree as a reference guide, rather than some abstract and abstruse handbook on implementing good governance. Yet this mesh of connections is ignored, in favour of more technical and 'practical' solutions that may make sense to the head but never to the heart.

The centrality of connections came home to me one day when I was dawdling around the police-training centre. Some police officers, who I knew, were outside a classroom, having a smoke break. Inside they were being trained on how to use *Analyst's Notebook*, an expensive software program that enabled the user to map out the familial, financial, and other connections between, for example, an individual and a group. The officers were neither impressed nor inspired by the application, which had come lauded by, among others, the US army and the FBI.

The policemen didn't see the point. They said they knew all the connections already. What was the need for writing them down? I don't know for sure, but I'm fairly confident that somewhere in police headquarters there are two boxes filled with the CDs for the software package, gathering dust.

One tawdry corruption case, which would eventually ensnare Lucia Lobato, was an especially clear window onto this world of connections and conspiracy. The case involved alleged kickbacks on a fuel contract won by her husband, and it played out for months over the pages of *Tempo Semanal*, a rambunctious weekly newspaper that delights in exposing the petty and not-so-petty corruptions and abuses of power in the post-independence government. The story was a long-winded 'he said'/'she said' tale, complete with pictures of aggrieved protagonists smoking cigarettes and looking as if they'd been photographed mid-complaint, along with photocopies of smudged contract documents allegedly falsified in Lucia's ministry, and demands from all and sundry that there should be an 'investigation' by 'competent authorities'.

'I am calling on the government to carry out a profound investigation,' said Joao Alves, the chubby, aggrieved co-owner of the company that had won the contract, but which was somehow duped out of the ownership owing to a document switch-a-roo allegedly perpetrated by the minister's husband. The aggrieved minister was standing by her man: she blamed the chief prosecutor for over-politicising the case, allegedly acting on a tip-off from the president. Bad blood had apparently been engendered somewhere along the line during a high-stakes poker game held at the minister's house.

The story was byzantine in its complexity, and I got the sense that the first act hadn't started that year, but many years before. The only way that I could possibly rationalise it was to draw a diagram and, as well as the formal titles, use personal relationships and party affiliations to establish the links between people. What I drew was as ungainly as a child's scrawl, but only then did it seem to make a lot more sense. The president and the prosecutor were formerly married, and the complainant was from the same party as the prosecutor. The prosecutor and the minister apparently thoroughly dislike each other. All this left me none-the-wiser as to whether Lucia's husband was guilty of anything, or whether she had conspired to assist him, but at least it explained that the politics were more akin to a family drama than many of the protagonists had made it out to be.

The case eventually ended up in court. Parliament voted to strip Lucia Lobato of immunity from prosecution; among the most forceful advocates of this course of action were representatives of her own party. I tried to get an interview with Lucia, but her chief-of-staff told me to write her a letter requesting a meeting and to ensure that the letter contained appropriate salutations.

I'd lived there long enough to know that the letter trick was a classic brush-off technique. In fact, Lucia was using the same technique to extend her stay in office. She had maintained that legally correct channels hadn't delivered the letter she had in fact received about her immunity being taken away. She was eventually convicted, and appealed to the prime minister to save her from jail. She occasionally popped up on Facebook, bemoaning (seemingly entirely without irony) the weaknesses in the Timorese justice system. At the time of writing, Lucia was in jail, but doing her damndest to get out. She claimed she was suffering from high blood pressure, and needed treatment abroad. (A chronic allergic reaction to Timorese prisons appears something of a family trait.)

Another inmate in the prison system is a fraudster from god-knows-where in sub-Saharan Africa who, perplexingly, claims he is Timorese, despite fairly certain visual evidence to the contrary. Before his sentence, he had been running — irony of ironies — an NGO campaigning for honesty and transparency in Timorese politics.

And what of Nicolau's son, who was but a babe-in-arms in 1975? The child lived and had grown up with relatives in — of all places — Jakarta. His name is Jose, and he is now country manager for Conoco Philips, one of the resource companies drawing gas from the Timor Sea and providing revenue on which the country depends to build its future. He now works for one of the oil companies that his father went to lobby in 1975. The more one looks, the more one sees connections. I asked Rogerio about this, and he smiled and uttered a Portuguese phrase: '*Somos todos primos*.' ('We are all cousins'.) Life and politics in this land of magical goats is about alliances and friendship, a world away from the technical approaches outlined in the jargon-filled handbooks of the international development community. Even though that's a general rule around much of the world, it's not one that obviously guides how development bureaucrats appear to think about places like Timor-Leste and how they structure their interventions.

When I left Rogerio's office, his outside porch was thronged with men who said they were ready to lend support to their candidate. One supplicant told me he was the brightest and the most worldly of all the candidates. I replied that some people overseas might have found this potential turnaround from jailbird to candidate baffling, perhaps even a little distasteful. 'This is not Australia,' he said. 'You need to understand that.' He was right. We look for people with familiar titles, but think too little about who people are, where they come from, and what they have been through. In the end, Rogerio came fifth out of a field of thirteen, polling much better than pundits had predicted. He is the consummate survivor.

Chapter Three

Down from the Mountains

Among the most striking pieces of footage smuggled out by foreign journalists from Timor during the Indonesian occupation were grainy pictures of wild-looking men perched on high mountain outcroppings, speaking in Portuguese and vowing to die rather than accept rule from Jakarta. They wore their hair long, and never cut it for fear that doing so would diminish their ability to deflect bullets. In their pockets, many carried the bark of sacred trees that they believed would keep them safe. Before a battle, they would chew the bark into a wad, spit it on their hands, and slather the mixture of bark and spittle onto their faces — an emolument that they believed made them invisible. Others carried *rai lakan*, a stone struck by lightning that sanctified it to deflect bullets. Others wore a crocodile tooth around their necks for added spiritual protection. The weapons that they carried were trophies of past battles. The soldiers marked the resting place of the dead with stones so that they could come back when the war was over and re-bury the deceased closer to their family's spirit houses.

These men were the soldiers of FALINTIL (The Armed Forces for the National Liberation of Timor-Leste). FALINTIL was the armed wing of the resistance that fought a lonely struggle over twenty-four years against the Indonesians. It was created as the armed muscle of the political party FRETILIN; in the short days of sovereignty in 1975, its members constituted the armed forces of the new state of Timor-Leste. The Mozambican leader, Samora Machel, provided them with their first uniforms as his gift to mark Timorese independence. During the early years of the occupation, FALINTIL controlled a significant portion of the country. But as Indonesian control strengthened, the fighters were pushed eastwards, and their activities were driven underground — their tactics changed from those of an army to those of a 'hit-and-run' guerrilla force. Hopelessly outnumbered, though sheltered by many in the community, they were spied upon by others. The soldiers were frequently starving, and many times lived off little more than berries, roots, and grubs. Only a few wore shoes. They rarely had access to pharmaceutical drugs to treat their wounds, and relied instead on traditional medicine, making use of ground leaves, seeds, and grubs. Bullets remained lodged under their skin for years; in fact, their bodies still bear the physical marks of those tough times.

The current prime minster and long-time leader of FALINTIL, Xanana Gusmao, has a bad back, owing to years of sleeping on rocks, and sometimes he finds it difficult to walk because of the pain. One fighter with reputed supernatural powers, who went on to become a member of parliament, Cornelio Gama, has four stumps in place of fingers on one hand. I got to know him a little bit during my time in the country. Indeed, in quite possibly one of the oddest things I've ever done, the two of us once went together as part of a delegation to Hawaii for a leisurely three-day meeting that included a concert performance by 1980s crooner Glenn Medeiros where I manfully, if probably unsuccessfully, tried to translate Medeiros' global hit 'Nothing's Going to Change My Love for You' into Tetun for him.

Our plush hotel on Waikiki beach was a world away from

FALINTIL's sleeping arrangements when they fought the Indonesians. The fighters lived in rough, damp jungle camps and caves that they shared with clouds of bats and rats that nibbled on them when they slept. I once panted up a steep hill outside of Viqueque to visit one of their hideouts and, as I ascended, regretted every cigarette I'd ever smoked. My guide was a teenage boy wearing an old Real Madrid shirt and ragged jeans with a red star stitched on the left leg at the knee. About halfway to our destination, the boy threw his flip-flops behind a rock, saying it was easier to walk barefoot, and he laughed good-naturedly as I kept slipping, sliding, and falling on the muddy track. He had an encyclopaedic knowledge of the names, battles, and occurrences that were fresh in his mind, even though many of the events he described had happened years before he was born.

After hours of trudging, we reached our destination. We squeezed through the entrance to the cave and, as we went from one cavern to another, I realised that there was little chance I would have been able to find my way out of this place without guidance. My life was totally in the hands of this young man. 'FALINTIL lived for months at a time here,' he said, using a cigarette lighter to partially illuminate the darkness as the bats screeched above us and the flame flickered. Now I could see why so many of the FALINTIL had nicknames that were variants on the word 'Niki', the Tetun word for 'bat'. As we left, we both touched the feet of the statue to the Virgin Mary in the small grotto that was built outside. On the walk down, my guide asked me if I had heard the ghosts of dead soldiers talking to us inside the cave.

Gama had lived in this cave. So, too, had Falur Rete Laek, the former Indonesian army militia commander turned FALINTIL fighter, on whose family's lands we were walking. He was a reputed sorcerer, who during resistance times went off into the forest at night to sing magical incantations. Falur was a man who had acquired an unlikely godson along the way — a man known by the name 'Niki Mutin' (White Bat), an Australian who showed up in Timor in the late 1990s to fight for independence and who sounded like a one-man international brigade. He'd been christened high up a mountain peak in central Timor, his original birth name washed away and replaced with his baptismal name, Jose Antonio Maria Raul. Purportedly on a secret mission, he was originally suspected of being a spy or hit man, but was eventually accepted by the FALINTIL and lived with them. Stories of his exploits are now recounted and retold into myths and legends, and we talked about him on the way down. Why and how he ended up in occupied Timor remained a matter of fierce conjecture; did the Australians, Americans, or even the Israelis send him? No one really seemed to know that, or even his real name. I also heard he had a long criminal record and had many outstanding warrants against him. I heard, too, that he had acquired supernatural protection that kept him safe, and that he'd once made himself invisible to avoid being stabbed by a double-crossing Timorese killer. As we walked, my guide told me that White Bat spoke multiple languages, including Makassae, a complicated tonal language spoken in the Viqueque district and across the east of the country. His Portuguese was more fluent than even the president of Portugal, he told me, somewhat improbably. He was reputedly a master of disguise, and had the power to change shapes and form. My guide spoke of him with reverence and asked if I knew him, as if it were the most normal thing in the world that two people living in Australia should be acquainted.

The boy's story intrigued me — so much so that I was determined to meet this Swiss Army knife of a man. But my quest to find the White Bat was not an easy one; even after spending about a year or so making various inquiries about him, I drew a total blank. At one point, I was forwarded an email that he'd written to a man who was inquiring on my behalf. In it, he wrote that this part of his life was over and that he wanted to move on. A shame, I thought, and began to move on, too. Then, one day when I was on the way to pick up my son from childcare, a phone number rang that I didn't recognise. I picked it up. 'Hello, mate,' said the voice. 'My name is Jimmy, but you probably know me better as the White Bat.' He told me he wanted to tell his story before he died. I asked him how old he was. He was thirty-nine years old.

At the time, he lived in a little town called Mount Beauty in the snowfields of Victoria, and I drove there to meet him. He was a well-built man dressed in black gym gear who had red hair and a greying beard. He was anxious to talk.

White Bat had earned his *nom de guerre* on account of his fondness for snoozing during the day. 'We couldn't sleep at night because that was the most likely time for anyone to attack, and so what else was I to do?' he said, not unreasonably. His pillow was a Tetun-language book written by an eminent Australian professor called Geoffrey Hull. Over ten years on, he said he still didn't sleep well at nights — a fact I can attest to, given that he went to sleep at one in the morning, but I was woken from my slumbers on the couch a bare three hours later as he padded around, putting wood on the fire.

I thought the stories about the arrest warrants must have been overblown, but White Bat assured me they were true, too. He had fifteen outstanding warrants in Australia against him for, among other things, home invasion, grievous bodily harm, kidnapping, and armed robbery. The White Bat never would tell me how exactly he'd ended up there — he said he was sent on a mission to build something he obliquely referred to as 'it' — but his tales of nearly two years immersed with the FALINTIL fighters in their claustrophobic jungle camps were both so fantastical and so lurid that I doubted that anyone could have made them up. We had spent the previous evening barrelling through a carton of mid-strength Australian beer, with one extraordinary story following the other. There were tales of drinking warrior's potions, killing giant anacondas, stripping weaponry, more about building 'it', and rugby-tackling a deer. The next morning, he went on to tell me about a monkey trained to kill humans once given to Falur as a dubious gift, a man with very sharp teeth leashed like a dog, and the paranoid atmosphere of the jungle camps where dead leaders appeared at night. White Bat had indeed, he himself believed, once become invisible in order to evade an assassin, and had been transported to a mountain hill. His stories sounded like a *Boy's Own Story* spliced with *Heart of Darkness*. Perhaps the most gloomy thing about our conversations were his recounts of the poor mental and physical shape of his comrades after the war was over, impaired as they were by alcohol and gambling. 'Many of my Timorese friends are damaged people,' he said, staring into the fire. He himself felt he'd only emerged on the other side after many years in the darkness, and that was why he felt able only now to talk to me.

FALINTIL had maintained the flickering flame of independence in the face of extraordinary adversity, wrenching family circumstances, and terrible personal cost. The experiences that these resistance fighters had lived through were so visceral and traumatic that they did not prepare the men well, either for later service in the army of the state that they helped to found, or for a return to civilian life.

The man who led many of the foreign journalists to get their stories and film the FALINTIL on lung-bursting journeys up steep mountain passes, like the one I walked, was Jose Antonio

Belo. Acknowledged in nearly every book written about Timor over the last twenty years, he is now director of *Tempo Semanal*, Timor's leading investigative newspaper. Jose is a good-natured troublemaker, single-minded in his pursuit of what he thinks is right. His office is any one of the coffee shops of Dili, and his phone is constantly jangling and beeping with news. His eyes sparkle with excitement when he gets a new nugget of information. He has sources everywhere: from the boys who sell cigarettes and phone credit on the side of the road, to government ministers keen to cast an unfavourable light on a colleague. His paper and website publishes page after page of allegations about craven civil servants and ministers. He runs tales of missing money, suspicious rice contracts, and apparent contraventions of procurement laws. His stock-in-trade is the scanned copy of a secret government contract that he shouldn't have access to, or copies of text messages sent to someone else that he shouldn't have read. He makes people in positions of power feel uncomfortable. Lucia Lobato threatened to sue him for defamation and to throw him in jail for publishing texts from a mobile phone that she had mislaid and which ended up in his possession. When UN police questioned him for some infraction, he rigged up a banner outside UN headquarters that said, 'You can kill the newsman but not the news.' Ministers call him and plead with him not to publish harmful stories, but their entreaties have no impact. His tough, shared history with the men in the mountains probably helps keep him safe. Jose is a close friend of mine, and he is among the people I admire most in the country. He was the cameraman for my marriage in Dili in 2010. I've even managed to forgive him for accidentally wiping half of the wedding video.

He is remarkably cheery and uncomplicated for a man who has led so traumatic a life. He was born in Baucau, but as a toddler he and his family fled to the mountains to escape the Indonesian invasion. He told me he didn't want to tell me what his first memory of Indonesians soldiers was, but I read elsewhere that he'd been forced to watch them do unspeakable things. The family was dirt poor and he moved to Dili, working as a houseboy for a wealthy Timorese family. He slept on the porch outside and ate one meal a day, a regimen that he still maintains.

I remember Jose telling me once that he had three ambitions while growing up: to learn very good English, to go to jail, and to be a journalist. He has achieved all three. He learned his English from an Australian nun, and she was a good teacher — he is fluent for someone who has spent comparatively little time in English-speaking countries, and is rarely stuck for a phrase or expression. He spent a total of five years in prison. In 1991, Jose witnessed the Santa Cruz massacre and was imprisoned soon afterward, hung by the feet from the rafters. At different points during his imprisonments, he was tortured with electric shocks and beaten by Timorese members of the local Indonesian police, some of whom went on to wear the uniforms of the police of the newly independent Timor-Leste. Years afterwards, he went to Jakarta to interview one of his chief torturers, now a leading businessman in Indonesia, in one of those rapprochements that demonstrate how much I'll never understand the place.

Only a fraction of the news material that Jose helped shoot made its way to Western TV screens. To go through his jumbled 'archive' is an exercise in comparing and contrasting what was said about independence when it was a faint dream for the men in the mountains and what has happened since. Jose took many recordings of David Alex, the former regional commander of the FALINTIL who died in an ambush that some suspect may have been set up by jealous comrades in the late 1990s. David Alex's is a voice from the grave, and it warns the military not to get involved in politics. The man who replaced him is called Taur Matan Ruak (which in English translates as 'the man with two sharp eyes'). He is now the president.

Timor's conflict was pre-digital, and these recordings are shards of documentary evidence in a struggle that has no agreed history. The Timorese resistance was national in aspiration but secret and segmented in operation, with little communication between its various parts. The result was a lack of interpersonal trust, and endless intrigues and conspiracies that are entirely understandable, given that some men who unconditionally served the cause also betrayed it. Alarico Fernandes, the minister of information and internal security in the short-lived government of 1975, surrendered with his weapons and the army's last remaining radio in 1978. If one of the most ideologically staunch members of FALINTIL could do such a thing, clearly no one could be fully trusted. Uncertainties created mistrust and rumours surrounding intentions and stories of those who had disappeared or died during the conflict. These accusations and hard feelings did not end with independence. Modern Timorese political lives are grounded in resistance heritage and have long, unseen, and gnarled roots.

In the end, the FALINTIL helped win independence by abstaining from the fight. They cantoned themselves in advance of the 1999 referendum vote on independence, maintaining their ceasefire despite seeing and hearing their countrymen being killed. It was an act of extraordinary discipline and self-control.

In February 2001, Jose filmed the ceremony when the FALINTIL became the official armed forces of the new state. Taur Matan Ruak became head of the defence forces, and Lere his deputy, but there was much dissatisfaction and allegations of chicanery and political favouritism in the selection procedures.

Bureaucratically, selection was based on technical requirements of experience, health, and capability. However, subjective criteria also appeared to play an important role. The process for integrating personnel from the resistance movement into the new force was not transparent; all decisions regarding who would become part of the army were taken alone by the FALINTIL high command and Xanana Gusmao. The leadership cadre seemed highly biased towards people who came from three home districts in the east of the country, and the decision to exclude the majority of FALINTIL from the new defence force provoked fury among those who were left out. All the men thought of themselves as being soldiers, but soon found out they were no longer considered to be so. I remembered something that White Bat had told me: 'In the jungle, if you were missing part of an arm, you could still carry a weapon.' Yet now, his friends found themselves surplus to requirements. Some of those fighters denied entry vented their frustration by rampaging through the camp where they had been cantoned during the two-year wait, destroying their possessions in the process.

The name FALINTIL lived on in the new defence force (the ungainly FALINTIL–Defence Forces of Timor-Leste is surely a candidate for any longest military-title award going around), as did the Portuguese-era ranks and appellations, but the leaders struggled to fit into very different roles. The ideal of independence was one thing; the reality, quite another. Hiding out in the forest practising guerrilla warfare did not prepare them well for working in an office, developing a budget, or writing policies and procedures. Running an army required new styles of leadership, management, and discipline that many of the ageing combatants found difficult to acquire. Another problem was that there was not enough work to fill their days. As FALINTIL troops, they had shaken off the Indonesians; but, now, as the national army, their major threat was boredom. The risk of an invasion was extremely small. These were men in a job, but with very, very little to do. Day followed day with little activity to fill it. They struggled for relevance, and the role of the army seemed to have slipped a long way down the priority list of former resistance leaders in a chaotic time of political transition.

Some military leaders took out their frustrations on the younger soldiers, particularly those recruits who came from the western districts out of which FALINTIL had been squeezed in the early years of the occupation. The commanders spoke to the recruits in their languages of the east, knowing that their Fataluku and Makassae could not be understood. When they did use Tetun, they spoke coarsely and condescendingly. 'You Westerners did nothing,' I was told they'd said. 'You would have shit yourselves if you had had to fight. I bet you can't even fuck properly.' The young soldiers murmured about and texted every graceless word to each other, with each re-telling inflaming their sense of grievance. They complained that they were overlooked for promotions, and that when there was a training opportunity or a foreign trip, their names were replaced by less qualified people with family connections to the leaders. And when the young soldiers returned home, they were met with laments from the FALINTIL who had not even been selected to join the new force.

Workplace bullying, boredom, a breakdown in the military structure, and low wages that were barely enough to cover travel costs to and from the barracks to their family was a combustible mix. Their frustration festered for years until, in early 2006, the soldiers from the western districts drafted a letter to the president and prime minister, asking them to look at the problems within the army. Their aim, they said, was to draw the leaders' attention to problems within the force, not in order to destroy the force but to repair it from within. They shared draft after draft with each other, and argued over the text. The group was called 'the petitioners', but only one person dared to sign the letter — a young lieutenant from the cloud-covered hills of Ermera, called Gastao Salsinha. The commanders, he wrote, 'do not implement the spirit of consolidation' and instead practise the 'spirit of divisionism', and he listed thirty-plus incidents of alleged insults, bullying, discrimination, and unbalanced administrative favouritism that he'd been told of in the previous six months. He typed his letter on one of the few functioning computers in the compound and sent his letter to the president, the prime minister, ministers of interior and defence, heads of the military and police, the church, and the embassies in Dili. Then he waited.

He did not receive a single written reply. This snub only added to the men's sense of disregard and discontent. More and more of them joined the ranks of their cousins and friends, and a month later, nearly six hundred soldiers walked out. Some were more aggrieved than others. 'I went because all my friends were going, and I would have been the only one left,' said Longuinhos, a somewhat melancholy, tall, thin, twenty-year-old who had formerly been a bodyguard to Commander Taur Matan Ruak. We met under the shade of a casuarina tree in Atabae, a town halfway between Dili and the border. He was driving a motorbike taxi in the mornings, and using the proceeds to buy palm wine to get blotto in the afternoons.

To compound the situation, the government decided to summarily sack the soldiers for abandoning their posts. In response, Salsinha led hundreds of the ex-soldiers, still in uniforms but without arms, to a protest in front of the *Palacio do Governo*. Relatives, sympathisers, and groups with grand names such as the Front for Justice and Peace, which were mainly fronts for various opposition parties, joined their ranks. Their numbers swelled further with the hundreds of unemployed youth that milled around the centre of Dili each day. The demonstration was a good way of breaking the monotony of the average day.

The petitioners and their supporters hoped that they'd somehow persuade members of the government to enter into a conversation with them in order to discuss their concerns and resolve the problem. They were to be disappointed. Day after day, they saw government ministers and their acolytes driving to the office in the morning and leaving at night. No one came down the steps to talk to them. Five days in the broiling heat inflamed already hot tempers. Rioting broke out on the fifth day of the demonstration, and the army was called in to restore order. The petitioners' former colleagues were now firing on them.

The events in front of the Palacio uncorked mayhem. Neighbour burned neighbour out of their homes, the army re-armed old veterans with evocative nicknames such as Van Damme, Lito Rambo, and Oan Kiak (Poor Child) to go against groups with names like 7–7, 5–5, and 3–3, so named for the number of ritual marks branded onto the follower's body. A maze of other martial-arts groups, street gangs, and youth associations fought turf wars and seemed to be on different sides at different times. Politicians, police officers, and soldiers seemed to be involved in many groups, and sometimes more than one at a time. There was a profound regional split. Timorese were stopped at checkpoints and asked if they came from the east or the west; their answer determined if they were allowed to pass. Jose Belo told me he feared that soldiers from the west would shoot at him because he came from the east. Some Timorese believed that the nation was suffering because their ancestors had laid a curse on the living.

At the same time, senior members of the military who had been giving support to the petitioners left the army in solidarity. They included a darling of the Australian army, Major Alfredo Reinado from the Military Police, who was seen as a future military leader. Reinado had movie-star looks, a radiant charisma that inspired devotion in his followers, and an erratic style that meant no one was ever entirely sure what he was going to do next. He was originally sent out by the F–FDTL to contain the petitioners, but he ended by going on the run with them as their leader.

No one was safe. As well as the conflict between parts of the army, there was a conflict between parts of the police and also between the police and the army. Pitched battles were waged throughout Dili. Matan Ruak's house was attacked by a member of parliament. Some of the petitioners and ex-FALINTIL attacked the military headquarters. The Pakistani police chief of the UNPOL mission was shot at as he attempted to negotiate safe passage for Timorese police officers who were hemmed into their headquarters by soldiers. He survived. Nine Timorese police were less fortunate. Meanwhile, Rogerio Lobato was arming a shady militia led by a former FALINTIL soldier who went by the perplexing nickname of Rai Los (True Land). Minister Lobato, wearing a flak jacket, arrived at one point at police headquarters, bellowing, 'Kill them all.' There was a feeling of utter lawlessness. There was no one to call for help. The country's police and the military were not just incapable of controlling crime and lawlessness; they were complicit in fomenting it. The situation was so bad that the government requested an Australian-led peacekeeping force and an international policing presence to come in to restore immediate public order. Under great pressure, the prime minister resigned, reluctantly.

If this sounds confusing, it was. A series of events seemed to happen all at once, but they are so murky and confusing that almost everyone, apparently, had a different version of where, when, or how the events of 2006 occurred. It is like a Timorese Rubik's cube that I have never managed to put together. Even now, trying to understand the motivations of the myriad actors involved and the politics that underlay it all brings exhaustion but little clarity.

Within the space of a few months, many of the national institutions established by the UN and subsequently handed over to the government upon restoration of independence in 2002 had unravelled. Bad blood between Prime Minister Mari Alkatiri and President Xanana Gusmao paralysed the government. The crisis exposed the fact that there was little of substance to the security forces beyond their guns and uniforms. The tensions laid bare cracks that had been papered over between and within the political elite, the police, and the security forces, and demonstrated how family ties trumped institutions. Lino Saldanha, the deputy police commander, left his post and joined his cousins in the F–FDTL. (Earlier in the year, Lino had apparently attended a month-long course on 'good practice in the security sector'.)

When I went to Timor-Leste in 2007, the police and the military were still very much in a 'daggers-drawn' posture. The United Nations had returned a year earlier to police an uneasy peace and to build police capacity — something they had so obviously failed to do in previous missions. Unfortunately, their basic model of doing so had not changed, making renewed failure likely. They also had a mandate to assist the Timorese to review their security structures. In one of the early meetings I attended to review these structures, I got my first inkling of how difficult success would be to accomplish. In a set-piece workshop led by UN staff with simultaneous translation headphones, the police and the military were asked to develop 'action plans' for reform. The result was a lot of steely looks and stares, and formulaic responses written on butcher's paper almost designed to be thrown away. The international staff, their ID cards dangling ostentatiously around their necks, tended to keep to themselves during the coffee breaks. They were unable to talk to almost all of the Timorese they were paid to 'advise'. One man who looked especially disdainful throughout was a prominent commander called Lere Anan Timur, a man who has led a life that is the stuff of nightmares. During the invasion, fellow Timorese reportedly betrayed his father. Each of his brothers and a sister were all killed during the war, and his newborn son was raised by Indonesian soldiers — the very soldiers who'd been bent on killing him. When father and son were reunited for the first time, they met through a translator, as the two did not share a common language. Lere wore a taciturn expression throughout. The foreigners who offered plentiful advice now had been conspicuously absent during the long, hungry years in the bush. The workshop broke up with vague promises to have another one. Neither the police nor the military talked to each other as they left the meeting.

Meanwhile, up in the hills, Alfredo Reinado was giving swaggering interviews to journalists. They had seemed to find him relatively easily, even though the government insisted that he could not be located. 'I'm happy up here, I can get a pizza and a cappuccino if I want,' he bragged to one Australian camera crew as he and his band struck appropriately martial poses for the cameras. He spoke with the oratorical flourish of a Latin American revolutionary. He invoked 'the people' and 'justice', but his words served to tantalise rather than to clarify. One of his favourite lines was that he could not give up his gun because it was not his gun; it was the people's gun. This makes less and less sense, the more you run the phrase around in your mind.

'It was really exciting, like being in a Hollywood movie,' recalled Tito, who was one of Alfredo's bodyguards but is now studying political science at the National University in Dili. The story of

Alfredo had a plot that became more melodramatic with each passing month. It seemed Alfredo had broken out of prison with the aid of magic, mysteriously opening doors and, along the way, acquiring a girlfriend called Angelita Pires, whose siren beauty had turned the head of every senior politician in the country. Villagers feted him wherever he went, and, at one point, some village leaders bestowed him with paranormal powers. He was involved in a series of circular dialogues with senior politicians about 'justice' and other such vague topics that were mediated and paid for by Swiss peaceniks. His old shooting buddy, the prosecutor-general, Longuinhos Monteiro, issued him a safe travel pass so that he could travel anywhere at will without fear of apprehension. The government paid many of his bills and expenses. He slept many nights in the Maubisse Pousada, at that time one of the most comfortable hotels outside Dili.

In the meantime, down in the capital, the international response consisted almost entirely of macro-level committees and reviews that addressed policies alone and remained oblivious to the personalities involved. Despite the pre-eminence of politics and personal histories, 'reform' was approached and explained as if it were a purely mechanical exercise. The histories that joined and separated the various parties were often not known or simply disregarded, with the result that the international approach generated amusing anecdotes but few results.

I wish I'd kept better notes of some of the meetings that I attended, as they were howlingly funny in terms of their po-faced absurdity. When I worked as a consultant with the UN mission, we went off to see the grandly named 'Presidential Committee on Reforming the Security Sector'. To all intents and purposes, this was a job-creation scheme for former government ministers who hadn't engaged in very much reform when they had been in office and for some Portuguese advisers who had been attached to the president's office. Roque Rodrigues led the committee. He was a wispy-bearded Maoist, one of the revolutionaries of 1975, and, most recently, the secretary of state for defence who had been fingered in the commission of inquiry for sanctioning the distribution of weapons.

The committee also included Alcino Baris, the man who replaced Rogerio Lobato as minister of the interior. Their recent pasts weren't mentioned. Instead, we engaged in general collegiate chit-chat about the need to reform security structures and develop policies. Although the military and police had been invited, they did not show up, giving the discussions an air of unreality. The meeting dragged on for hours. Both the UN and the Timorese were solicitous in saying that they did not want to be the first in preparing a 'reform plan', but I think that this was more because neither side had the first clue as to what to do. At the end of the meeting, I cadged a smoke from Alcino Baris, who told me that it was imperative that Timor developed a national-security policy. I agreed but asked, if it was so important, how come he hadn't worked on one when he was in office. He said that was a good point. I came away from the meeting with the sense that we had spent the afternoon ventilating futility. Yet my colleagues from the UN divined that we had made 'policy gains', and wrote a glowing report to send up the bureaucratic chain.

Eventually, the Timorese soldiers and police reconciled in a way that made sense to the Timorese, but much less to people like me. The impetus was not a law, or a policy, or a committee, or a long meeting, but a shooting. On 11 February 2008, the president was badly wounded in a shooting incident in which Alfredo and one of his men were killed. An hour later, Prime Minister Xanana Gusmao was fired on, but escaped injury. Those basic facts are clear, but everything else that happened is surrounded in a mist of claim and counter-claim. Some say that Alfredo went down to shoot the president; others say he was lured there on the pretence of a meeting in order to be gunned down. Angelita made him do it, said some. Gusmao and/or Ramos-Horta arranged it all, declared others. The assault on the prime minister didn't happen; but, if it did, he managed to evade capture by changing shape into a white dog, was another explanation. If you asked ten people, you got ten different answers. Each sounded entirely reasonable until another came along that was even more persuasively complicated than the last.

The evidence trail was contradictory. If anyone should have known what happened, it should have been Marcelo Caetano. He was the man charged with shooting the president. I decided to go and ask him.

Arranging the meeting was an extravaganza of cloak-and-dagger secrecy. A friend of mine arranged it all and said that he'd contact me with details of the 'secure place' in which I'd meet Marcelo. I was told to make certain I told no one about the meeting. I wasn't at all sure where he was going to summon me, but I certainly wasn't expecting it to be a seamy ex-pat-from-Down Under hangout in the capital called One More Bar — the sort of place that Crocodile Dundee would make his watering hole if he lived in Dili. The location turned out to be an inspired choice, though, as it was a quiet place to talk. Save for a few blotchy-faced drunks watching re-runs of Australian sport and a Filipino tattooist called Two Lights sizing up an expat for a 'tribal art' tattoo, we were the only people there that afternoon.

I didn't recognise the man who arrived at the bar, although his top-of-the-range motorbike he parked just outside should probably have tipped me off that this was someone of import. I'd only previously seen pictures of his face wearing war paint and a tight hat, and he had filled out a bit since then. 'The journalists would love it if I looked kind of mean,' he said by way of reasonable explanation. It was just after noon and he was hungry, so I suggested that we order food. The first problem was that the menu was in English, and the second was that there was no rice in the kitchen. He was thoroughly perplexed by my explanations of scampi, sausages, salads, and other Western pub-food staples. 'You *malae* don't eat rice with each meal?' he asked, his eyes wide. 'No,' I replied, although assuring him that I really did like rice very much indeed. 'That's very strange,' he answered, shaking his head in childlike wonder. He said that I was the first foreigner with whom he had ever had a conversation. He lived in a completely separate world from the foreigners in his midst.

Eventually, we settled on a cheeseburger and some fries. We talked about his home high in the mountains in Atsabe and the story of the Bandera waterfall, the place that many believe is the high watermark established when the sea was so high that a whale had swum up to the mountains. The local people had a sacred sword and spear that God had given them, and they used the weapons to kill the beast and cause the waters to recede. By a strange coincidence, he shared the name of the last military leader in Portugal before the 1974 revolution, and I asked him if he was named after him. He thought it unlikely; his parents, he believed, had never read a newspaper.

Marcelo insisted that I smoke one of his clove cigarettes as he started with his story, which I remember to have been lucid, persuasive, heartfelt, and stirring. But reading my notes later showed me that he had not said anything of substance, and in fact I learned little more than what I had already known. He spoke with Alfredo's histrionic style, and did not fasten his discourse to names and facts: 'We fought for justice because we were suffering; we are the sufferers; we submitted ourselves to justice because we love this beloved country. I would not hurt anyone as we all love our land.' He wasn't being evasive, and he wasn't being unhelpful — this was just the way he talked. To my Western-wired brain, his words had little or no content; to him, they made perfect sense.

He didn't seem to know why Alfredo had decided to go down to Dili, either, or why he himself had been accused of shooting the president. (The president said he remembered Marcelo shooting him, but later said his memory was faulty.) 'As I said in court, I stood guard over the president when he slept in front of me when we were having all those dialogues. I didn't kill him then, so why would I shoot him later?' he reasoned, opening up another pack of cigarettes. He believed that someone else, a member of the elite, knew the story of that day, but it wasn't him. After spending three hours talking in detail with this man, I was none the wiser as to what had happened.

'I just don't know how the president was shot,' he told me before roaring off on his motorbike, which, to complicate matters further still, had apparently been given to him as a gift from the state intelligence service.

Regardless of the identity of the shooter, the attacks were a game-changer. Ramos-Horta was rushed to Darwin for emergency surgery and, less than two years after firing on each other, the military and the police formed a 'joint command' to chase down the renegade soldiers — including Marcelo, who had fled back to Ermera and sheltered in the homes of relatives. It was a peculiar operation. The United Nations were legally in charge of policing, but both they and the Australian–New Zealand military peacekeepers were sidelined. The United Nations police commissioner did not return any earlier from a very important meeting in Italy he was attending; the rebels eventually came down from the mountains without a shot being fired; and the chiefs of police and defence posed with rebel leaders for various 'thumbs-up' happy-snap pictures. When they came down to Dili, the rebels handed their weapons to the deputy prime minister and sundry members of the political elite, and, following that, all went off for a roaring party where everyone got drunk and many danced till dawn. Marcelo struck me as a man clearly fond of dancing and carousing, and he said the party was one of the best he'd ever attended. There was nothing in the hefty international handbooks on best practice in the security sector about any of this sort of stuff.

Few of those investigated for the events of either 2006 or 2008 went to jail. Marcelo Caetano was found not guilty by the court, and the president subsequently pardoned those who were convicted. Timor is such a small place that you end up bumping into some of the protagonists regularly. The shady former paramilitary leader Rai Los is a regular patron at Hotel Timor, owns a large construction company, and is an influential member of the governing party. To my surprise, in the course of writing this book, he invited me to be his Facebook friend. Out of curiosity, I accepted, to find that, according to his profile, he likes horror movies and Cristiano Ronaldo.

I got talking to a bit-part player, Antonio da Cruz, in the course of an extraordinarily boring meeting on community policing, a favoured initiative of donors. When my eyes didn't spark with recognition as he introduced himself, he suggested that I go off to read the United Nations Commission of Inquiry into the events of 2006, 'because I am famous'. I went and re-read it, learning that he was the man who Rogerio Lobato had tasked with distributing weapons from the police armoury. He had duly handed over the arms to Rai Los, in a graveyard, in the dead of night — for a bit of dramatic flourish. When I rang him up later that day to say that I now knew who he was, he was as pleased as punch with his infamy. I asked him what he was doing now, and he mumbled something about being in charge of police discipline. Every time I saw him subsequently he never failed to give me a big wave.

As for others, I once met Oan Kiak at the top of the Cristo Rei monument in Dili, where he had just finished his morning stroll ... Lino Saldanha carried the Timorese flag at the Olympics in Beijing and is now commander of the police maritime unit ... and Angelita married her Australian lawyer, and now lives with him in Darwin. When the lawyer's ex-wife discovered that he was leaving her for Angelita, she attacked him with a samurai sword. Angelita later ran for the presidency and came last.

None of the bigger fry have been prosecuted for their role in the 2006 crisis. Investigations were delayed, and cases quietly dropped. Even old, implacable enemies are being rehabilitated. Alarico Fernandes, the man who betrayed the FALINTIL in 1978, returned to Dili in 2010 to a hero's welcome. It's a full-time job keeping up with the break-ups and rapprochements, and trying to winkle out the underlying logic to it all. Perhaps there is none. Often, it seems that the only ideology is opportunism.

Marcelo seemed to be doing pretty well for himself, but what about the rest of the petitioners? In 2008, they'd been paid US$8,500 each by the government and told to return to civilian life. What were they doing now? A few years on from the crisis, I went to find out. The man helping me with the research was Egidio, the cousin of a man who I used to work with. I'd suggested that we meet at Hotel Timor; but, as soon as Egidio walked into the coffee shop, he recommended we go elsewhere. He knew too many people there, and he didn't feel comfortable talking around them. We went back to One More Bar. Egidio seemed to have the number of every petitioner on his battered old Nokia phone, and if he didn't have an up-to-date contact, his friend Nelson did. Egidio knew no English, and Nelson knew only two words, 'peace building', which he'd learned when he worked for the NGO World Vision.

The two men were great researchers and relished the opportunity to do something interesting for a few weeks, make a bit of money, and have the chance to go off and see their buddies. We discovered that many of the petitioners had returned to relative obscurity, although they still enjoyed the cachet of their previous designations. About half of them seemed to be scratching around Dili, doing nothing in particular, with the remainder back home in their districts, passing the days in doing very little. The money they had received as compensation was long gone. Some had used the windfall to build a house. Many had bought motorbikes, now defunct, fancy mobile phones, and gifts for girlfriends that they no longer had. Only a small minority were making a return on their money in small kiosks and shops. Some had used it to buy a ticket for Northern Ireland.

We met at a variety of locations, but their stories were remarkably similar and as vague as those of Marcelo. 'The problems aren't resolved and we still don't have justice,' they said, reciting old slogans about injustice without really thinking what they meant. Leaders in the army didn't speak *lian los*, the true word. 'But we're good friends with everyone now again,' many said. They missed the camaraderie and kudos of being in the army. All but one I met wanted to rejoin the organisation they'd spent the previous hour lambasting. I looked baffled. How could they think that would be wise when the protests they initiated had led to a complete breakdown in law and order? They didn't seem to think it would be a problem. 'In Timor, we get hot quickly, but we cool off quickly, too,' Egidio explained. Again, such reasoning made no sense to me, though it undoubtedly made a lot of sense to them.

Gastao Salsinha, the lieutenant who had signed the letter that started all the trouble, cast a shadow over all these conversations. Everyone we met spoke of this man with reverence, respect, and deference. 'To receive the full story, you must talk to our commander, Lieutenant Gastao,' almost all of them said. My two research assistants would ring him most nights for no purpose, other than to say they had called, putting the call on speakerphone so that I could hear his voice, to demonstrate that they were close to a man of authority. When I went to his house expecting to meet a frothing revolutionary, I found instead a very quiet man. He was wearing an orange T-shirt proclaiming the virtues of community radio, and his kids played peek-a-boo from behind the door. He spoke softly with a shy smile and did not resemble the angry-looking guy who I had previously seen in newspaper pictures and on television. He scowled only once, and that was when I asked to take his picture. I told him that he reminded me of my father, who also glowers every time he gets his picture taken — he even grimaced in his own wedding pictures, while my mother smiled like a basket of chips beside him. 'I know how he feels,' Salsinha said. 'I always tense up in front of the camera.'

He had never left Timor-Leste, but said he'd like to visit Australia so that his children could see some of the wildlife. He found it incredible that people came from all over the world to hear his views. He was interviewed by *The New York Times* ('I am told it is famous'), and had once been door-stopped by a Thai television crew that had driven up the windy road from Dili to solicit his views on the Red-Shirt movement that, at the time, thronged the streets of Bangkok. He had never heard of the movement, so he made some stuff up. Nowadays, he tries to keep a low profile. 'That Jose Belo is always calling me looking for a *Tempo Semanal* exclusive, but every time I talk it causes me trouble, so I try not to say anything.'

He asked me what I had found the most surprising thing in the course of my meander around the country in search of the ex-petitioners. I told him how the lack of animosity between former petitioners and current members of the Timorese military astounded me. They waved at each other when they saw each other on the road, attended each other's family ceremonies, and generally got along like the best of friends. He found it amazing that I found *that* amazing, and recalled the long and amicable card games he'd played with his captors after he was arrested. Our exchange seemed to capture the quintessential oddness of the place.

He, too, seemed to have no animosity towards his soldier colleagues, although he was happy to be living away from the deal-making and politics of Dili. He had more cause to be cynical about politics than most, and recalled a conversation that he had had with Ramos-Horta just before he was pardoned. The president peppered him with questions. Who funded you? What did Angelita Pires do? What was this person doing? Ramos-Horta praised Salsinha for not saying anything during the trial. 'I'm going to pardon all you petitioners, and that will be the end of it.' Salsinha didn't think that this was fair and said he told Ramos-Horta so. He believed that the politicians should also go on trial. 'You are really, really stupid if you think that's going to happen,' snapped Ramos-Horta. 'The big leaders played us like cards,' Salsinha said forlornly.

As I drove back down to Dili from Salsinha's home, a truck of the Timorese defence force zoomed past me on a tight bend. I wondered why they needed to drive so fast. They seemed to have nothing very much to do when they reached their ultimate destination. The army was now back to pre-crisis numbers, and their salaries had improved, but many soldiers continued to be without activities or tasks to animate their working days.

A friend who visited them out on the border said that they spent their days helping to carry wood for the local farmers. On the day I visited, the soldiers were whiling away their time playing chess. The army has bought two enormous boats from China to patrol the seas and has ordered some more, and requested helicopters, but the issue remains as to what a defence force that faces no threat is meant to do on a day-to-day basis. The issue of relevance is implicit, but rarely is it directly addressed. Perhaps arising from its resistance heritage there seems a general air of untouchability about the F–FDTL. Stories about the deeds of officers are whispered, not reported.

One man prepared to respectfully and politely ask difficult questions about the army is another Belo. He also comes from the town of Baucau. His name is Nelson and, although unrelated, he knows Jose Belo very well; they used to play together as boys. Although very different in temperament, they are both — in their own ways — dedicated to following David Alex's edicts. Jose does it through his breathless exclusives, and Nelson through running an NGO dedicated to security issues. His yearly budget is comfortably smaller than the salary of a foreign-born media adviser to the Timorese police whom I knew, whose specialty was taking out-of-focus pictures.

Nelson's NGO is called Fundasaun Mahein (the Guardian Foundation) and it pumps out research pieces and publishes reports on developments concerning the police and the military. The reports are polite and respectful, but come often with a quiet punch: why is there no obvious separation of tasks between military and police; why are the police so militarised; are the boats that were bought really the most effective use of resources? The reports are written in Tetun and Indonesian, and digested and discussed by far more people than are reports written by Western researchers, myself included. He and his staff speak with a moral authority that comes from lived experience as a Timorese and a background working for the resistance.

Like Jose, Nelson's cheery disposition disguises a traumatic past. He was a student activist and, again, like Jose, he was arrested in the aftermath of the Santa Cruz massacre and tortured in the Komarka, the now-defunct Portuguese-era prison that is directly across the road from Fundasaun Mahein's poky offices. Nelson was moved from prison to prison for six months after the massacre, during which time his family did not know if he was alive or dead. He learned good English which, when the UN and international troops arrived in 1999, was a skill much sought after. He worked as the translator for Peter Cosgrove, the head of the Australian peacekeeping forces that arrived in 1999. Nelson remembers visiting him subsequently in his home in Sydney, sipping iced tea on his lawn, and sailing on his boat in Darling Harbour. He was a long way from his small home in Baucau.

Fundasaun Mahein was certainly not a get-rich-quick scheme. Nelson earned a fraction of what a good English-speaker could have earned as an adviser to the government or in the undefined 'business' activities that seemed to have engaged many of his contemporaries. It is early days for his NGO, and it faces some significant challenges: many of the researchers lacked basic research skills when they arrived; they cannot read the laws because they exist only in Portuguese; and their funding is not lucrative enough to hire more experienced staff or to expand their presence beyond Dili. But they understand the backstory of the way that political decisions are made in and for the security sector. And their workrate is prodigious: detailed reports are released at least once a month. Covering the walls in Fundasaun Mahein's modest office are framed pictures of the men in the forest. The dead fighters stare down at them, lending spiritual encouragement to their work.

Chapter Four

Ghosts of the Past

The old Ministry of the Interior building where Rogerio Lobato once ordered police guns to be distributed to his hand-picked goons is now almost unrecognisable. A university library in Indonesian times, the building has been renovated extensively and renamed the Secretariat of State for Security. It is as if the government wants to clean away all vestiges of the old rogue. To what extent the redecorations are built to last is open to debate. The electric 'self-opening' doors at the entrance didn't work without a button being pressed, and the lights in the toilets didn't switch on, necessitating an extremely accurate aim that most men don't have. The smell of urine was pervasive. Then there were the missing links on the rickety staircase rails that could easily catch out an unwary visitor.

Despite the changes, the statutory function of the office remains the same: it is to provide civilian oversight of the police. This is a difficult job in any country, but especially so in this place where allegiances to constitutional provisions are not necessarily strong enough to override other ties. The job is difficult for the person at the top, Francisco da Costa Guterres. He is a small, urbane, sometimes puckish man entering his fifties who dedicated his PhD to the former resistance leader and current prime minister, Xanana Gusmao. When Francisco took over the job, he said his handover from his predecessor consisted of just one page — an out-of-date organisational chart of the office structure.

There is certainly a lot more paperwork in the office now. Francisco's king-sized office table is covered with piles of paper, and the office bookshelves are filled with neatly organised binders. A didgeridoo, the gift of an Australian minister who came up on a 'meet-and-greet' visit, lies forgotten in a corner. The gift was a last-minute replacement when the visiting party realised that the 'Timorese picture' they had originally intended to give was actually one of the Solomon Islands.

Five years in the job had aged Francisco. His smile beamed out of his inauguration photo, but the hair was less thick now and his eyes had bags beneath them. He looked like a man in need of a long holiday. His three phones beeped and rang throughout the three-or-so hours I spent with him, and he said that they were rarely silent for long.

No wonder he was tired. He probably had one of the toughest jobs in the government, with problems coming at him from all directions.

First, he had to deal with a non-performing and under-motivated bureaucracy. Signs accompanied by clip-art images saying, 'I am embarrassed when I arrive late and leave early', which are posted on every office door, result in neither personal humiliation nor improved punctuality. When I worked there, civil servants would regularly doze at their desks or stare blankly at the screen, sometimes moving the cursor around in a circular motion as if stirring a cup of tea. The arrival of the Internet on office computers was not a boon for productivity. Facebook replaced solitaire as a way to while away the hours.

The *funcionarios* seemed happier driving the new state cars than steering any particular policy agenda. Many struggled educationally.

According to the government's own documentation, three-quarters have only secondary-school qualifications. Many lack the numeric skills necessary to handle large budgets; donors grumble behind closed doors that the bloated civil service is more akin to a state welfare system than a service-delivery mechanism. As a result, the ministers have to rely on national Timorese advisers who are often better educated and better paid, solving to some extent the problem of getting things done in the short term, but doing nothing to increase productivity in the longer term. The civil servants grumble that the national advisers only have the job because they are relatives, friends, or former colleagues, and complain about their salary packages. It is a vicious circle guaranteed only to erode the state budget ever more quickly and to entrench ever more deeply the petty jealousies about money and rank. Francisco's office is the reality of what the handbooks, guides, articles, and concept notes refer to elliptically as the 'challenges' and 'complexities' of establishing effective and efficient public services in new states.

Second, Francisco had to deal with a police institution that did not necessarily want to be overseen. The Timorese police seemed more interested in the provision of material goodies than anything else. Seemingly, no number of cars, motorbikes, bicycles, new buildings, or electrical equipment could satiate their appetite. I told Francisco about how I had been told by one senior officer that he couldn't engage meaningfully with the community until the government bought him a karaoke machine and sound system. Francisco laughed hollowly. He had heard many more outrageous requests than that, and he may very well have funded some of them. Although his office had developed many new laws and regulations (many written by Portuguese advisers, not by the Timorese themselves), the problem was in entrenching them. Joint UN–Timorese government assessment teams found that policies, procedures, and processes within the Timorese police were either non-existent, not known, or not being followed.

Impunity and non-accountability within the police remains obvious. The Timorese police seem reluctant to sanction their own: when I left, there was an average of one disciplinary case being mounted for every 2.5 officers on the force, and cases would languish for years without resolution. Personality politics also played their part. Many believed that problems between this office and the police were exacerbated because Francisco did not get on well with the police chief, Longuinhos. The two rarely met of their own volition. It seemed there were never enough months in the year to include a picture of the other person in their respective glossy office calendars.

His problems of the present are complicated by his past. During Indonesian times, he was a senior functionary in the Indonesian administration and a member of a political grouping called the East Timor People's Front that was associated with some extremely nasty actions at the end of the Indonesian occupation. Although he himself is not directly accused of these deeds, his association with them is indelible, no matter what he tries to do. He jumped ship — or, more accurately, he says, publicly identified with the vessel that he was backing all along. In 1999, when the Timorese voted for independence, he acted as a go-between — leveraging his English to liaise with international donors, and using his political connections — to connect militia leaders with Taur Matan Ruak and the FALINTIL fighters. He was not the only one to change with the prevailing wind. Many of the supporters of autonomy are today working for and saluting the flag of the sovereign state that, less than fifteen years before, they fervently agitated against. One apparently super-rich former minister, Gil Alves, made his money from being close to the Indonesian military and executing their contracts during the Indonesian period. He was a spokesman for the militias in 1999.

The head of the Timorese football association, once a former contractor for the Indonesian army, was a money-man for the governing party and, in the last election, became a minister. (His most newsworthy contribution since assuming the portfolio was to make the case for Timor-Leste hosting a Miss World competition.) Whether as ministers, businessmen, or hangers-on, many of the autonomy supporters seem to be doing extremely well in independent Timor-Leste, prompting frustration from many old veterans who felt they gave the best years of their lives for an independence from which they are not reaping the benefits.

Neither was it just the elite who expressed discontent. Significant numbers of Timorese worked for, or were co-opted into working for, the Indonesians. They were employed as civil servants and police officers, or as eyes and ears. Bishop Carlos Belo was famously reported as having said that, during Indonesian times, Timor was a paranoid place where 50 per cent of the population was informing on the other 50 per cent. In the 1999 referendum, over 20 per cent of eligible voters opted for the territory to remain as an autonomous part of Indonesia. In the immediate aftermath of the violence that followed the publication of the result, many fled over the border into Indonesian West Timor. But over the last decade, most people have returned — many to the same villages where they lived before.

Although the occupation is over, its legacy remains. When I went to Timor in 2007 to do a research project on veterans, I remember hearing them contrast their lot as 'winners' with that of the 'losers'. I recall that the men became particularly fired up about those people whom the Indonesians had supported through university and postgraduate education, many of whom were now in the

government, to be seen riding high in air-conditioned 4WD cars
with tinted windows, while the less fortunate populace lived in
miserable shacks and scratched around with no money.

Having come from a country with much more entrenched
identities, I was always surprised by the malleability of the Timorese
elite — the more so, given how much the people had lost. Relations
with Indonesia were a case in point. No one knows for sure, but
the accepted figure is that over one hundred thousand Timorese
died in conflict-related deaths during the occupation. Despite
that figure, independent Timor-Leste has very rosy relations with
its former suppressor. Both ex-president Ramos-Horta and the
current prime minister, who both spent the best years of their lives
fighting *against* Indonesia, now take every opportunity to speak
in terms of forgiveness; successive Timorese governments have
shown no interest in pursuing serious charges against suspected
war criminals. The push to forgive and forget is couched in terms
of pragmatism and psychological mending. The Timorese have
chosen not to pursue cases against either the Indonesians or their
local militia proxies, even though both stand accused of a catalogue
of murders, rapes, and exterminations. When a member of one of
the militias, Maternus Bere, was arrested in Timor-Leste in 2009,
he was subsequently released into Indonesian custody, and he now
lives in freedom.

Political reconciliation trumps prosecutorial justice every time,
according to former president Jose Ramos-Horta, who delights in
telling Western human-rights advocates who lobby for indictments
that they are not living in the real world. Prime Minister Xanana
Gusmao — a man captured and jailed by the Indonesians — has
even publicly hugged some of the generals who spent years trying
to capture or kill him. It followed that supporting Indonesia during
the occupation was clearly no bar to serving in Prime Minister

Gusmao's cabinet or to making money. But, at the same time, past associations have not been scrubbed clean. Countless times, I heard police officers and civil servants grumble elliptically about Francisco's background.

Perhaps it is these close connections between families and the suffocating nature of life that so inhibits international efforts to bring perpetrators to justice. The Timorese government has been implacably opposed to efforts to pursue and prosecute fellow Timorese (and Indonesians) alleged to have committed atrocities during the conflict. The reluctance to prosecute Indonesians can be explained by the *realpolitik* of not wishing to enrage a larger neighbour, and many of the Timorese suspects are now also Indonesian citizens. However, it is also difficult to go against family, especially in this place where family is so important. Almost everyone has a brother, sister, or cousin who supported autonomy and, in the craziness of 1999, was complicit in acts of medieval violence.

I liked Francisco and enjoyed working with him, so I thought he'd be the best person to ask about how autonomy supporters were faring in his newly independent state. I had known him for years, but had never talked about the issue directly. Consequently, I spent the first twenty minutes of the meeting pussy-footing around. If I, as a *malae*, was having difficulty addressing the matter, I could see why the Timorese — with so much more at stake — found it even more difficult. But when I eventually broached the topic, I felt I had breached a dam. He talked faster than I could take down notes. We were meant to meet for half an hour, but our conversation ran on and on. While what he said both surprised and perplexed me, it made sense at a human level. Looking back, given what we now know, we academics and researchers may have been assigning too much ideology to something that was inherently pragmatic. He said his decision to work with the Indonesians was for the most prosaic of reasons: he needed a job and he needed the money. Moreover, he had an advantage over others looking for the position: his cousin was a member of the Indonesian parliament, and managed to open doors that for others would have remained closed. Another cousin was the administrator of his home region, Viqueque. He had windows into two worlds. Looking back, he says that he was never really a staunch supporter of the Indonesians. His cousin Carlos, who had the winning nickname 'Freezip', was a founder member of the Timorese student movement with Fernando 'La Sama' and Lucia Lobato. What he was describing was not uncharacteristic. Almost all families were divided by the Indonesian occupation. One brother might have supported independence; another might have been feeding information to the Indonesians.

Perhaps it was the gnarled family connections and friendships that explained this accommodation of such mobile loyalties. In a place in which family is so intrinsic, almost everyone was connected to someone who had been on the side of integration. No Timorese family had entirely 'clean hands'. It's easy to hate someone in the abstract, but much less easy when you know that person is a school friend or one of your own. Perhaps, also, in a small, tightly knit society there is less room for grand principle. Xanana Gusmao made a decision that his new state couldn't run at all without an educated corps, and that he couldn't afford to antagonise the Indonesians. Small societies offer no place for moral absolutes, and every place for political flexibilities.

Further evidence of this was to be found down one flight of stairs from Francisco's well-appointed office, where the National Directorate for Prevention of Community Conflicts was situated — a body that does much less than its grandiloquent name would suggest. Originally, the title was probably devised because it sounded so good and was the equivalent of a 'come and get me' title for donors with buckets of money they were anxious to spend on projects marked 'peace building', 'conflict resolution', and 'stability' — phrases that are too sweeping and broad-ranging to capture the very familial nature of Timor's conflicts.

I worked with the office in its first years and helped develop all the accoutrements of what we, as internationals, think a modern department should have: vision statements, mission goals, newsletters, quarterly plans, and reporting regimes. The idea, looking back, was probably hopelessly optimistic, and it broke down almost immediately. According to the plan, the ostentatiously named directorate would hire Timorese civilians drawn from each district who would work as 'focal points' and report on conflict 'trends' in their districts, sending back the information that was then to be processed into a database in Dili and packaged into a report for members of the government. At an intellectual level, it sort of made sense; at a practical level, it turned out to be too complicated and, well, required a more consistent degree of application than was able to be realised.

It took more than a year to hire the 'focal points', and then there was no money to train them. There was then the issue of how to categorise concepts such as 'conflict'. This was followed by the question of who was going to develop the training package; no one in the office was capable of undertaking this role. There followed debate about funding for phone credit and fuel for the workers' motor bicycles. It took nearly an equal amount of time to chug through the UN system to approve the funding — one sticking point was insistence from the directorate that a sound system and a computer be added to the price tag — and when that was eventually agreed, it took another few months to round up the signatures. Any original impetus had long evaporated by the time the first report was produced, which then, apparently, sat in the secretary of state's office for a few months, rendering the information completely out of date. It's lucky the prime minister and his colleagues relied on information garnered much more from gossip, rumours, and flurries of text messages from their network of contacts, associates, and hangers-on than on the content of these reports. It may very well have been my Tetun, but somehow what I was trying to engineer seemed totally alien to the Timorese. We were trying to bureaucratise and complicate the way by which information flowed, and were attempting to rationalise decision-making in a place where politics and conflict were personal. Nor were we the only ones doing so. All too many of the schemes I heard about seemed to take insufficient heed of the complications of competence, capability, and personal interests.

Some time during this period, I came to an epiphany. The purpose of this bureaucratic appendix was less to prevent any particular conflict, and more to prevent the civil servants and their extended families from falling into poverty. In reality, this was as good a place as any for civil servants to spend their days in return for getting paid. It may not have started out that way, but it was little more than a job-creation scheme with added access to state cars, rather than a particular initiative to prevent conflict. I was, to use a generous definition of the term, working inside an office that seemed to encapsulate what donors carefully describe as having 'little local capacity'. Even if they had possessed the interest, the civil servants simply did not have the basic educational building blocks necessary to perform the tasks that were expected of them. Eventually, I gave up pushing the bureaucratic rock uphill and instead marvelled at how days and weeks could go by without anything very much occurring, and how this relative indolence was then rewarded by foreign donors who went weak at the knees at the sound of a sexy institutional title. One day, the entire directorate trooped off to Okinawa for a three-week course on peace building. They came back frothing with outrage about the continuing US naval presence on the Japanese island. Northern Ireland was floated as a destination they might like to go to, as many family members now lived there.

The directorate was headed by a woman called Lidia Lopes de Carvalho, who came from the mountain region of Ainaro and a town called Cassa that was synonymous with a pro-Indonesian militia called the MAHIDI (an acronym which, spelled out in English, meant 'Dead or Alive, for Integration with Indonesia'). Two brothers called Nemesio and Cancio headed the militia. They popped up regularly in journalist accounts about 1999, as they gave good copy to newspapermen and delivered reliably bloodthirsty rhetoric into cameras on a regular basis.

In the run-up to the referendum, the MAHIDI and other militias with equally bellicose names burned down the houses of reputed supporters of independence, and carried out a series of attacks across the territory, often under the noses of the Indonesian army and police, who claimed to have been powerless to stop them. However, subsequent evidence confirms the close and near-symbiotic relationship between them. According to both journalistic and scholarly accounts, Indonesia armed, supported, and paid for the militias, often using death, coercion, and threats as recruiting techniques to compel membership. Cancio and Nemesio Carvalho stand accused of a catalogue of grisly crimes; their indictment lists multiple murders, abductions, house burnings, and forced repatriations. Cancio is reported to have ordered militiamen to point their guns at a heavily pregnant woman and open fire. Someone told me once that he'd then wrenched the foetus from her womb — although that, surely, was a *danse macabre* flourish too far?

Lidia is Cancio's and Nemesio's sister. This sibling of the two brothers who laid waste to whole villages is the woman charged with preventing community conflict, hawking applications to donors for peace-building funds, and getting disconcerted at Yankee neo-colonialism. As if to prove how the occupation divided families, she married a pro-independence supporter. I always quite liked Lidia, even though I could not always induce her into following the work plan. She seemed to quite like me, and when I left the program she showed up with a *tais*, a traditional Timorese scarf for me to keep as a memento. When my son was born, I received a text message from her which said that I had received a great blessing from God.

The more I read about the activities of the Carvalho brothers, the more I wanted to see for myself what they were both like, and hoped she could facilitate an introduction. Both had fled over the border with the Indonesians in 1999. Cancio still lives in Kupang, in Indonesian West Timor. Nemesio — the self-styled intellectual of the group with a degree from a leading Indonesian university and an apparent penchant for sprinkling his conversations with lines from William Shakespeare — returned back home a few years later. The charges against him were dropped, and he returned to living in the family home in Cassa, where he worked as some sort of coordinator for the Democratic Party, a group of activists who fought and agitated for Timorese independence, who were now entering middle age. He'd been a schoolmate of the party's president, Fernando 'La Sama', and their friendship endured despite their diametrically opposite political positions. I'd also heard he'd advised the rebel leader, Alfredo Reinado, about political strategy. The younger Carvalho's political life seemed to encapsulate the unconventional nature of politics in the country, and it seemed incredible to me that he was living in plain sight with a clean judicial slate. I resolved to try to meet him.

So, after meeting Francisco, I toddled warily downstairs to Lidia's office, knocked on the door, and asked her if I could I speak to her about a sensitive matter. She shooed out the civil servants and, after they had closed the door, I asked her if she could she arrange a meeting with Nemesio. 'Sure thing,' she said, and promptly dialled his number, putting the handset onto speakerphone so I could hear the conversation.

'My colleague Sr Gordon wants to meet you,' she told him. 'He lives in Australia, and he's writing a book. He's a nice guy. His son has a Tetun name.'

'That's good,' he boomed down the tinny speaker. He was happy to meet. She wished me good luck and said she'd endeavour to track down Cancio. When I came out of Lidia's office, it was apparent that almost everyone else had been been straining to hear our conversation. They all quickly feigned being hard at work, but the game was somewhat given away by one of the civil servants reading a piece of paper that was upside down, with his 'letters in' and 'letters out' trays sitting empty on his desk.

The next day, I hired a car and drove down what the Timorese call the *super mie* road, named for a popular brand of Indonesian instant noodles because of all the bends and twists in it. I drove past Dare and the memorial to the thousands of young Timorese who had lost their lives fighting alongside the Australian army during World War II. Just above it, I stopped to gape at work being done on a gaudy mansion. Apparently, it was being built by a senior member of the defence force. I wondered at how someone on a monthly salary of just over one thousand dollars could afford such a grand house. I asked the question of one of the builders, who was just putting the finishing touches to the front gates. He smiled. 'Oh, come on, *malae*, don't pretend that you don't know,' was his response.

I ran into the first major pothole about a mile from his house. It was about a metre deep, and there was no way around it, as the left part of the road had washed away entirely. Down I went, heart in mouth, but emerged unscathed. In the event of things to come, this deep hole turned out to be a minor inconvenience. For mile after mile, the gaps became even larger gaps with muddy tracks where the asphalt had long washed away. It was all-round driving treachery. At one point I came across a group of Timorese affecting to use a shovel and good-naturedly demanding a dollar before allowing the car to pass on towards the next driving obstacle. 'Why don't you call the government?' I asked them as I gave them some cash.

'No one will come,' said the old man, his lips rosy-red from betel nut. 'And, besides, we're enjoying all this money we're getting.' Eventually, the road improved, and I stopped every now and then at some old stone monuments and forts erected by the Portuguese that peeked out from many corners on the road. I enjoyed the solitude of it all. Travelling by myself, there was no one to roll their eyes at me stopping to take pictures of an overgrown fort. I stopped for cigarettes — which I knew were an essential smoky lubricant to all conversations in Timor — and lunch in Ainaro town, a quaint place that rose majestically out of the high mountain mist. Every second table in the Indonesian-style eatery seemed to have a snarling dog underneath it, so I opted for a takeaway. The owner shovelled rice, spinach, and a mangy piece of chicken into a plastic container, the contents of which I then ate on the steps just below a monument to Dom Alexio de Corte Real, the Portuguese regent of Ainaro during the Second World War who had apparently fought bravely against the Japanese. Legend has it that, when he was captured, he asked his firing squad to wrap his body in the Portuguese flag. His memorial was in serious need of repair. The four Portuguese crests on either side had been pecked off, and the paint of its inscription was close to fading away altogether.

A young man was lolling around as I ate, perhaps hoping I was going to give him a cigarette from the packet peeking from my trouser pocket. He asked me where I was going, and, after about five seconds of wondering whether I should fob him off with a white lie, I told him I was off to meet Nemesio Carvalho. He looked aghast. 'You can still hear some of the souls of their dead here at night,' he said. Timorese believe that the dead are not truly at rest until their bodies are interred back in their rightful, ancestral resting place. With at least some of the bodies of the victims of the MAHIDI group still missing, their families as yet are unable to give them a proper burial, and so believe that their souls haunt the mountainsides. As I drove down the valley for the remaining hour to Cassa, I began to feel queasy, either because of the lunch or the nature of the journey. On the way, I drove over a bridge from which the MAHIDI militia had thrown some Timorese they had identified as being supporters of independence.

After about an hour, I reached Cassa. It was an unremarkable town of palm-thatched huts and the odd concrete house, built on either side of the road at the bottom of a hill. I'd basically been descending since leaving Ainaro, and the temperature had risen dramatically. The town felt muggy but unusually busy. Taur Matan Ruak was in the town centre, meeting with veterans and trying to convince them to support his presidential campaign. Wardens milled around outside the venue, combining an air of jumpiness at having a dignitary in their midst with smug satisfaction at being in a position of authority for the day. Nemesio had told me that he lived opposite the police station; but, rather than ask one of the wardens for Nemesio by name, when they might have been on the other side of the political divide, I asked where the station was. This was a poor idea. They sent me in completely the wrong direction, perhaps out of mischief, but perhaps because they didn't know where the station was. I asked three other people, but they didn't seem to know either. This seemed to be a good-enough proxy indicator that the police were rarely called upon to do much. After about half an hour, I worked out that I'd passed by the station on the way into town; the little building was tucked in off the road, in the middle of a field of yellowing grass. In that field, Cancio Carvalho had allegedly strapped a supporter of independence onto a chair, poured kerosene over him, and set him alight.

If the story were true, he wouldn't have had far to walk to perform the incineration. The Carvalho homestead was just opposite the station. The homestead was an unremarkable whitewashed building, and a little boy was running around with a toy handgun on the patch of land outside it. His name was also Nemesio, and I asked him where his father was. Before his son could reply, his father appeared out of the homestead. He was a tall, handsome man in his mid-forties, with silvering hair and dancing eyes. He was much amused that someone had come down from Dili just to visit him. He was clearly glad to have different company, and confessed he was bored a lot of the time. He had planted sandalwood trees on hills just above the town, and told me he spent the days waiting for them to sprout. He invited me to sit on his porch, on a scoured, cream-coloured plastic chair that I was told had, over the years, supported Australian journalists, UN peacekeepers, rebel leaders, and an array of political figures.

I didn't know how to start the conversation, so I began somewhat erratically, chattering about the monument to Dom Alexio. 'That's all the Portuguese gave us, monuments and myths,' he said. 'Before the Indonesians came, many people here weren't wearing proper clothes and had no shoes. There were no roads. They were here four hundred years, and they gave us absolutely nothing. The Indonesians brought infrastructure, roads, and civilisation, but that wasn't enough for many Timorese. They wanted independence because they wanted titles and the power and kudos that came with it, and were much less interested in administration.' This was the widely held 'triumph-of-Indonesian-modernisation' thesis that I was often to hear from the militia leaders I was yet to meet. It was the popular diagnosis of the problems of present-day Timor. 'Look at this country now,' he said. 'It has more ministers and vice-ministers than even Australia has, and the roads are much worse than they used to be. But I'm a democrat', he continued with a grin. 'I must respect the people's decision.' As happened in so many of these conversations, members of his family sat by and listened in, nodding at each point he made. He was clearly the boss, and they — equally clearly — were the followers. I imagined that they would do anything he asked of them.

The evidence about what happened in 1999 points to a pre-conceived, well-planned scorched-earth policy, devised and instigated by the Indonesian army and indiscriminately implemented in part by their Timorese proxies. But Nemesio wasn't having any of this. He had his justifications and mitigating circumstances well honed and well prepared when I asked him about the bloody aftermath to the referendum. The violence was spontaneous, occasioned by the population's frustration with the United Nations. According to him, the UN had not reacted appropriately to reports of irregularities during the voting phase. It was all Kofi Annan's and senior UN officials' fault, and nothing to do with Nemesio. I told him I'd heard a lot about the militia intimidating supporters to cast their ballot for autonomy, and it not being the other way around. 'But that's my point exactly,' he exclaimed. 'The story has become changed by powerful people so that *our* story is discredited.' Like all good conspiracy theories, it was a hard one to refute.

The tale of his eventual non-prosecution tells of the human difficulties of separating professional from personal interests in a small place. International forces arrested Nemesio at the border immediately after his return, but he was quickly released on bail. The night he was freed, he had a lively dinner with friends, one of whom was the prosecutor pursuing his case. Maybe for that reason, his case never reached trial, and six years later it was dropped entirely, on the rather baffling grounds of lack of evidence. 'In point of fact, it was my human rights that were being infringed,' he said, referring to the length of time it had taken to conclude that he did not have a case to answer. His lawyer advised him to pursue a compensation claim. He seemed self-aware enough to laugh at the irony of launching an application, and opted not to.

It was pretty obvious that I wasn't going to unlock any revelations from him, if indeed he had any. He parried specific questions about the 1999 violence and the MAHIDI, answering in general, somewhat blustering, terms that reminded me a bit of the way that paramilitaries in Northern Ireland would bamboozle the press when they gave interviews. When the conversation was underway, I thought I was getting some new understanding, but when I looked at my notes later, all I had was page after page of circular statements that neither implicated anyone nor explained anything in particular. It was reminiscent in its vagueness of my conversation with the 'shooter of the president', Marcelo Caetano.

The conversation drifted onto the politics of present-day Timor, and I asked him who he supported politically. He answered by way of a story. 'Prime Minister Xanana, Taur Matan Ruak, and Fernando "La Sama" are on a desert island,' he said, 'and they only have enough food to enable one person to survive a week. A ship that will rescue them is that length of time away. "La Sama" says we should share the food and eat well for a few days, and he is sure that the ship will come early. Ruak says, let us remember the struggle that we had in the forest when we did not have enough food, and let us divide the food in three but eat small portions for the week — then we will be OK. Xanana says, I will eat the food myself.' I wasn't exactly sure what message I was meant to derive from this.

I'd put some packs of cigarettes and a lighter on the table. As was customary in this place of rigid social rules, people would then ask for permission from me before taking one and lighting up. We'd ploughed through about four packs when, suddenly, our conversation was interrupted by a bearded man with a bandana on his head, mascara smeared on his face, and a large cross around his neck. He was wearing a skin-tight black dress overlaid with a frilly purple rah-rah skirt. He pushed rudely between two of the men and made a grab for the cigarettes without going through the necessary etiquette. Nemesio's eyes narrowed at this infraction of protocol, and some of the men hustled him off. I asked who he was and what he was doing in that crazy get-up. 'Oh, he is a *komik* person,' explained Nemesio. It was one of those cases where a word with an English-language derivation has worked its way into Tetun, but it now meant 'a person with a serious mental illness' rather than someone who told jokes.

I asked what the man's story was. His parents had died during the occupation; he had seen them killed in front of his eyes. He probably needed care in a mental institution, but there was no such institution in Timor, and little prospect of one being built in the near future. Until a couple of years ago, there were no psychiatric beds in the entire country. Later, I was told that just US$12,000 of the government's budget in 2011 was dedicated to mental health.

So the deranged *komik* now roamed from house to house in Cassa, probably unsure of where he was, and potentially a danger to himself and to others.

It was clear for all to see how mentally broken-down the *komik* was, but what is perhaps less obvious — and what we, who come to the country sometimes don't see — is just how many Timorese have been damaged in a similar way by the occupation. Many of the men in Cassa have witnessed or heard things that are hard to stomach. Men and women have seen their children injured and raped, have lost sons and daughters, been tortured, been beaten, had their hands crushed, or been threatened at gunpoint. I preferred not to think that some of these things might very well have been done by some of the people I was talking to that afternoon. One study, conducted just after the independence vote, and reported in *The Lancet* in November 2000, indicated that more than one-fifth of all Timorese had witnessed the murder of a family member or friend. The researchers who conducted the study thought this might have been an underestimate. Given all this, and the fact that the bureaucratic world of strategic planning and administrative process demands very different talents from day-to-day survival skills, perhaps it's amazing that so many of the civil servants accomplish as much as they do. One study led by a team from the University of Auckland has suggested that as much as 5 per cent of the population suffers from Post-Traumatic Stress Disorder, with as many as 12 per cent exhibiting symptoms of psychosis. The overall message coming from a range of scholarly research conducted on the topic is that conflict-related mental illnesses are a public-health problem in Timor-Leste.

It was getting late, and I decided I wasn't going to risk driving back to Dili on the potholed roads in the dark. I drove back up the road for an hour, to Ainaro, and checked into the family house of the district administrator. (He rented out some of his front rooms.) I had arrived late, but managed to persuade his young daughter, who seemed to be acting in the role of hotel manager, to rustle up some fried noodles. I sat in the living room and waited for her to bring them out. It was a relatively opulent house in comparison to most, and each wall was adorned with graduation pictures of the family's children. Each graduand had clearly studied in Indonesia. Near my room there was a small altar with pictures of the recently ordained bishop of the area. During the occupation, the district administrator had worked for the Indonesians. He, too, had made a relatively soft landing in the new post-independence era. There seems no rhyme or reason behind a lot of the political pivots other than pure, hard-headed pragmatism. Some Timorese shifted political shape from *autonomista* to independence supporter as effortlessly as the *topasses* had changed alliances in days of old.

Back in Dili, pictures of the militia stared out from the photo exhibition in the Komarka, a former Portuguese-era jail that was taken over by the Indonesians and used for the same purpose during the occupation. Many of the people looked wild-eyed and almost delirious: it has been documented that Indonesian troops and intelligence officers jacked up their proxies on amphetamines so that they would feel neither fear nor a sense of right or wrong.

The former jail is now a museum in which visitors can walk through the cells and torture rooms. It is a fitting place to have housed the offices of the Timorese 'Truth and Reconciliation' Commission, known better by its Portuguese acronym, CAVR, which collected over 8,000 testimonies and interviews from victims and perpetrators, and produced a report of over 3,000 pages that serves as the most comprehensive analysis and oral history of the conflict.

In the early part of the last decade, the complex had been a hive of activity, packed with international experts, advisers, and consultants on 'truth telling', 'community healing', something called 'transitional justice', and other programatic reconciliation therapies. The new arrivals spoke in a sophisticated and reified vernacular — one that even many native English speakers would have found abstruse, and which went over the heads of many of the Timorese staff whose fancy-sounding titles did not necessarily reflect their educational levels nor relate to their job capabilities. The international staff had drawn their experience from other countries in which they had worked, or from the dense and tightly written textbooks they helped to write. Very few had had any direct experience of the horrors that they were helping to uncover. The huge disparity between their salary scales and those of the Timorese staff was also a source of much friction.

Like much of what was suggested to the Timorese by international bodies, and imposed upon them for no better reason than that there was the funding to do it, CAVR was a foreign import that tried to take root on Timorese soil. Tellingly, the final document is written in English with only summaries available in Tetun and Portuguese. (It was recently translated into Indonesian.)

The foreigners and their debates have left comparatively little trace. The CAVR complex is now a quiet, somewhat forlorn place, run by a skeleton staff and frequented only by the occasional foreign visitor. The last foreign staff member, an indomitable ex-seminarian called Pat Walsh, who dedicated much of his adult life to Timor and its people, left his position in 2010. The museum is closed on weekends and holidays — just the sort of days on which you'd think more people might have the time and inclination to visit it.

Reality has frustrated those who imagined that CAVR would be the springboard for something curative. Weighing in at over two thousand pages, the final report remains unread by many, and parliamentarians keep putting off debating its recommendations, which include seeking reparations from Indonesia. Even among my friends who seemed to lap up every piece of information about Timor-Leste, I could find no one who had read the document in its entirety. An academic researcher from the UK, who probed into the legacies of CAVR, found that very few victims were even familiar with the acronym, and far fewer knew what it was meant to accomplish. This is a powerful indication of the limits of wordy tomes in a society with high levels of illiteracy. It is also a reminder that we, who come to countries from outside, often bring highly censorious moral codes with us, perhaps because we are not dealing with our own countries. Reconciliation doesn't happen according to the neat time-frames of a funding agency. And revealing facts alone does not change a people's lot.

We do not perhaps see as clearly as we should that in small, isolated, tight-knit communities such as Cassa, victimisers, victims, and their families live close by each other and are often bound together because they have nowhere else to go. They will see each other almost every day and the approach of CAVR was, perhaps, too rigid, too rule-based; designed both in and for a place in which it is easy to get up and walk away. Truth and reconciliation appear somewhat too abstract and conceptually irrelevant, and they do not equate with the personal cadences of life. Messy local realities of mistrust, fear, betrayals, and survival sit uneasily upon, and are incompatible with, idealised goals devised far, far away.

On the way out of the prison museum, I got talking to some of the guards, one of whom had recognised me from when I had been working as a fixer to an Irish documentary crew that were filming in Santa Cruz, Dili's main cemetery. The graveyard had been the site of one of the most infamous massacres during the Indonesian occupation, which was captured on film and then smuggled out and broadcast around the world. The footage had helped to capture world attention and galvanise international action. In November 1991, Indonesian troops had opened fire on a student march just outside the cemetery. Over 270 Timorese were killed on that day, and yet not one was buried in the cemetery itself. Many of their bodies have still not been discovered. Some of the dead were thrown into the sea. Others were dumped in unmarked graves.

'You look a lot happier than when I last saw you,' the guard said. 'You seemed to be having problems with one of the crew ... the large one, with the white hair and the feet that became pink in the sun ...' The guard was either very perceptive, or my irritation with the brusque and charmless director of the documentary had been very transparent. The week of the filming had seemed to stretch on forever and, at one point, I remember thinking how awful it would have been to be stuck with this man for even a moment longer. But I was in the luxurious position of only having to spend seven days with him, although it felt like more. In small villages in Timor-Leste, there is no way to avoid people you don't want to see and who have done much, much worse than to develop a manner that is personally repulsive. For them, there is no international flight to get away on. 'I thought the Irish got along together?' he said, and I asked him where on earth he got that impression from. He said that was what his cousin, who lived in Northern Ireland, had told him.

The guard went on to ask if I knew of the case of the Timorese man who had been jailed in Northern Ireland for having stabbed his estranged wife to death and for then having attempted to do the same to her new partner. I told him I had heard about it on the news. The convicted Timorese was his childhood friend, and he tried to give me an explanation for the attack. 'He was shot and injured at Santa Cruz,' he said. 'He was never the same after that.

He suffered heavy trauma.' Timor-Leste's peace is underwritten with a deal to forgive and forget with Indonesia and to let the crimes done by Timorese unto Timorese slide by. It is one of the reasons that Nemesio and others have been allowed to come back home. But, behind it all, the ghosts of the occupation still haunt many.

Chapter Five
The Other Side of the Border

In my four years in Timor-Leste, I had probably spent about a total of four hours on the other side of the Indonesian border, driving on a transit visa through to the Oecusse enclave in West Timor. I was there again now.

To me, West Timor felt almost like the blank half of a map, even though over a million-and-a-half people lived there, comfortably more than the population on the eastern side. I had picked up little snatches of information, such as that it was the site of the once-great kingdom of Wehali that had stretched over most of the island before the arrival of the Portuguese and the Dutch. I also remembered the name of Kupang, now the provincial capital of Nusa Tenggara Timur Province. Captain Bligh had landed his ship near Kupang after an epic journey spanning nearly two thousand nautical miles. As a child, I had read about the event in a book, *The Mutiny on the Bounty*. But I knew very little about those Timorese people originally from the eastern part of the island who now lived on this side; in the years after the 1999 vote, nearly one-tenth of the entire population lived in the west. Many had been supporters of Indonesia and, with their families, had fled their homes, never to return. Some had allegedly been terrorised into leaving. I was familiar with the names of the notorious leaders such as Nemesio's brother Cancio, and Eurico Guterres, the leader of the largest militia known as Ai-Tarak (the Thorn). Eurico sounded like a Timorese version of Uday Hussein. I wanted to find out what had happened since. What were the leaders doing now? Did they want to return? Where were the Timorese living now? Nemesio told me that I should go and see for myself; so, after I returned from Cassa, I booked an air ticket to Bali and took an onward connection to Kupang city.

On the morning of my departure, in a slightly frazzled state at Denpasar airport, I started to seriously question the wisdom of the whole endeavour. My rough plan was to begin in Kupang and from there to travel to Atambua, the town near the frontier. But this was more a set of aspirations than a detailed itinerary. Somehow I had to figure out a way of meeting Maternus Bere, the infamous militia leader who had led the attack on the church in Suai. He had been arrested but then released by Timorese authorities who were fearful of the reaction of Indonesia if they kept him in jail.

I had the phone number of a woman who could act as a translator, and I had been introduced via Facebook to a woman whose husband was Filomeno de Jesus Hornay, a political supporter of autonomy and leading figure in UNTAS, the grandly named Union of Timorese Warriors. But that was the sum extent of my preparations. I spoke no Indonesian beyond knowing the numbers up to ten, and a few basic greetings. I potentially had many blank days ahead of me, and very little sense of how to fill them. I wondered apprehensively what men indicted for the vilest of crimes would make of an Irish guy they had never heard of popping in, unannounced, for a chat.

I spent the short flight fretting about what a monumentally and dangerous waste of time the trip was likely to be, but my worries seemed to evaporate as soon as I landed. I felt very much at home.

Kupang was like Dili's slightly scruffier older brother. Both cities were snarled with traffic, thronged with crammed mini-bus taxis plastered with early-career pictures of pop-nymphs such as Avril Lavigne and Britney Spears. Odd English phrases like 'infamy' and 'stairway to hell' were stickered onto the windscreens in such a way they almost fully obscured the driver's vision. I made a note to visit the factory that was producing this tat at some future point in my life.

Even the police uniforms looked very similar, right down to their toy-town badges. The architecture of official government buildings was indistinguishable from what I was used to in Dili. And inside, there seemed to be a similar inverse correlation between the amount of work being done and the number of people employed to do it.

The major dissimilarity was the lack of an international presence in Kupang, which meant that the cost of living was a lot lower. My $25-a-night hotel room would have cost at least five times as much in Dili. There were very few other foreigners around, and on a Friday night I visited Teddy's — a once-infamous beachside bar that I'd heard described as a sort-of Rick's café for Aussie expats. If Teddy's ever was that sort of place, it had clearly fallen on hard times. I found just two old leathery-skinned Aussies swearing and cursing in the corner about having been swindled out of a deal involving outboard motors. The perky young waitress said the pair had been hanging out there, carping about their grievance, every night for months. Nearly all life had long dwindled out of the bar. With the ending of the Darwin–Kupang air route, far fewer foreigners were coming to Kupang these days, she said. This was significantly reducing her chances of meeting a husband, she added sadly. Livid Bert and enraged Ernie in the corner were very slim pickings indeed. I stayed for just one beer and left. I think I spoke to only one foreigner in the whole time that I was there: a Swiss engineer who was staying in my hotel and who told me of the corruption and graft that he saw all around him.

'Kupang is certainly similar to Dili in some respects, but in a lot of ways it's a bit more old-fashioned also,' said Filomeno 'call me Meno' Hornay, when I met him in the smoky lobby of my hotel. 'This is a much more family-oriented place, and we don't have the moral degradation you see in Timor-Leste. We all go to church, for a start.'

Meno certainly did not look like a warrior. In fact, he was more the sort of man you'd find waxing lyrical in the campus bar. He had a master's degree in development studies from New Zealand, and he spoke easy, idiomatic English. He was the sort of urbane fellow who would have been an absolute darling of the donor set if he had been in Dili. His nephew was the anti-corruption commissioner there. Meno had been back and forth many times, and said he despaired of all the money being frittered away back in Timor-Leste on flash cars, aquariums, and other symbols of middle-class affluence.

I mentioned to him that the roads seemed, at first blush, very different and better in West Timor. 'They seem much better maintained, but they have less expensive cars on them,' I continued. His smile was rueful. 'In Timor-Leste,' he said, 'the Timorese don't like Indonesians, but they have learned corruption so well from them. I honestly don't know how some people can live with themselves with all the corruption that goes on over there.'

Meno was one of the self-styled intellectuals in the autonomy movement and was not directly associated with any violence. I asked him about what should be done with the 403 Timorese indicted by the UN and the Timorese authorities for what they had allegedly done. His answer was more forceful than the Timorese government's response. 'We have to accept that many of those who supported autonomy did commit crimes and that they should go for trial. But guilt didn't exist on one side only. If you killed someone, then it has to be proven, and you need to go to prison. But there are also people who killed and committed crimes amongst the pro-independents. How can you blame people from only one side and the other side be blameless?' Many of these men were now in the government. He said that he wanted to go back to Timor-Leste, but didn't want to feel fearful in his home.

So how did this seemingly reasonable and thoughtful man end up in the integrationist camp? His answer sounded like a dispassionate analysis delivered in a lecture room. He said, 'My country was weak in human resources, and there was no point in being independent in name only. Three years after the Indonesian invasion, there were roads and there was electricity. Was the occupation perfect? No, but I'm not sure independence is any better for people out in the mountains.'

He got fired up when I asked him about former colleagues who had been equally implacable in their opposition to independence at one time, but who now worked in the Timorese government. Some he mentioned who were now in government had been very strong pro-Indonesian supporters until just a few weeks before the referendum vote, but had then performed rapid 180-degree turns. 'I am a pro-integrationist. I did not change,' he said proudly, still seemingly shocked at their brazen opportunism, as if such political back-flipping had never happened before. There was something melancholy about him. He had the air of a forgotten exile who had been doomed to spend the rest of his days delivering a trenchant analysis that the government didn't want to hear, and was holding firm to a position that, financially, was probably not beneficial to him. He gave me two pages of phone numbers of people to contact, and wished me luck. He thought that many of the integrationists would be happy to tell their side of the story. 'Make sure you ask Eurico what he's up to,' he said. 'We elected him president of our association, but he takes the keys of the office with him every time he goes to Jakarta, and he hasn't put any of his money into it as yet.' The Timorese Warriors had apparently only gathered for one powwow in the last year. And, seemingly, they had only one set of keys.

Money didn't seem to be a problem to Eurico when I went to see him the next day inside his high-walled compound just outside town. His gaudy mansion was decorated in expensive, ageing-playboy chic, and I almost expected to find a caged tiger in the back garden. He wore a well-fitted shirt and an expensive jumbo-diamond-studded watch. A gigantic gold ring adorned with the colours of the Indonesian flag, which probably could have doubled as a knuckleduster, was on his other hand. His thick mane was tied in a ponytail, and extended all the way down his back. He reminded me of a well-built 1980s rock star. His lackeys included a portly man who wore a faded T-shirt of the US Christian rock-group Creed, and sported a top-of-the-range Nikon camera. 'I like to take pictures of all my visitors and put them in an album,' said Eurico with a wolfish grin. Indonesian pop starlets regularly called on him, my interpreter had told me just before we arrived. God only knows what sort of pictures are in that album.

He was enjoying the attention and playing up his infamy. He bellowed out gruff, bombastic, and self-regarding clichés as answers to my questions so quickly that it was difficult for my interpreter to keep up. It was almost as if he was speaking from a script. 'Autonomy was a middle ground to avoid conflict and victimhood; the violence was spontaneous; the UN should have anticipated violence, and so it is their fault, and they didn't confiscate weapons

…' Foolishly, at this point I somehow thought that we were going to have a rational conversation. 'But would you have given the guns to them?' I asked. He turned to his extensive collection of formulaic lines for a response. 'I cannot say, but I know that they should have done so for the sake of peace.'

More often than not, he talked about himself immodestly in the third person. 'In 1999, Pak Eurico came to Indonesia in order to save our people …' He rambled on and on. I underlined another phrase in my notebook as being especially memorable: 'Eurico cannot say that he is a hero only because he is too modest.' I asked him how he'd acquired sufficient wealth to build his house. He claimed that it came from two years' work as a security guard, and some lucky wagers.

Eurico was a mixture of the thoroughly cartoonish and the downright malevolent. Although he insisted we take goofy pictures beside some of his giant campaign posters that were planted inside the garden, he carried the air of someone capable of quick and easy violence.

He was just 28 years old in 1999, a former street fighter who had run rackets in Dili, in the pay of the Indonesian intelligence service. His life had been broken from an early age. His parents were murdered when he was a young boy, but the identity of the man who pulled the trigger seemed lost in the mists of rumour and counter-rumour. He said FRETILIN forces killed them, whereas some people in his home town said that the Indonesians killed them for being independence supporters. Eurico was subsequently brought up by an Indonesian civil servant.

Ironically, this man who later became a snarling poster-boy for Indonesia had started his career in the independence movement as a messenger-boy for resistance fighters. The writer Irena Cristalis relates a story about how a teenage Eurico was arrested for being part of a plot to blow up President Suharto's plane with black magic. Some accounts say that he joined in the Santa Cruz march in 1991, although he denied this was so in his usual third-person way of answering things: 'Pak Eurico was not there.'

With his mullet hair-do, baby-faced looks, and the swagger of a grenadier, Eurico was a media star back in 1999. He gave good copy to newspapermen, and was always happy to oblige by thundering bloodthirsty rhetoric to camera. (Later, I would meet his then interpreter — a man living in a small shack stacked high, oddly, with old school-exam papers — when he would tell me that it was the most exciting time of his life. 'BBC, CNN: they all wanted to talk to us!' he exclaimed.) The militia's former headquarters still stands. It is now a hotel called the Tropical, and it serves a gargantuan buffet each day that was especially popular with the United Nations police until the day they left at the end of 2012.

Eurico ordered deaths without compunction and sometimes in full view of the media. In April 1999, he was recorded telling thousands of militiamen gathered in Dili to kill pro-independence supporters. 'Capture and kill if you need' those who had 'betrayed integration,' he boomed, singling out the Carrascalaos, a prominent land-owning family. A few hours later, he led an attack on their house. Thirteen people died, and the perpetrators dumped the bodies into a well. At the very moment that Eurico was shooting through the Carrascalaos' windows, the Irish foreign minister, who had been visiting that day, was receiving assurances about the security situation from the governor.

The months in the run-up to the referendum were a blur of threats, accusations, shootings, rambling philosophising, stabbings, and dumped corpses, and Eurico's indictment ties him to many of these incidents. In the days after the referendum, Eurico and his men burned the centre of Dili down to a cinder. Eurico was commander of his own organisation, although he did not act alone; a series of detailed studies has laid out how his actions were carefully arranged in lockstep with Indonesian police and military commanders.

As we wandered around his lavish grounds taking pictures, I tried to broach these allegations. The indictment mentioned above is waiting for him in Dili should he ever return, although the case of Maternus Bere shows that this danger doesn't necessarily mean much anymore. I thought I'd toss him an innocent question to which you would have thought there could only have been one answer: had he anything to apologise for? He stopped, and his frown turned into a glower. He answered it by asking another question: 'Who is going to apologise to Pak Eurico?' If talking to Meno Hornay had felt like an exchange with a wise professor, a tête-à-tête with Eurico was akin to conversing with an out-there gang member.

While we were leaving the compound, my interpreter explained to me that Eurico has gone on to leverage his infamy into celebrity status in Indonesia. Pop stars call on him when in town, and he has apparently featured in a number of cheesy pop videos. He's a reliable B-list personality who will show up to an opening ceremony. My interpreter said that he sometimes pops up in gossip magazines. Everyone seems oddly tolerant of this former militia leader, as if he is no more than a good-natured rogue. Even former sworn enemies seem to accept him. I told a couple of Timorese who had been ardent fighters in the resistance movement that I had met him, and they asked if I had his phone number; they wanted to give him a ring and say hello.

Throughout my meetings in Kupang, I kept on meeting people who talked about how they were on familiar and friendly terms with the pro-independence leaders over the border. At another fancy house, another leader whose white eyebrows didn't match his hair told us how Gusmao and Ramos-Horta had told him that he and his followers would be welcome to return at the end of 2012, by which point the UN would have left and the indictments would be quietly forgotten. Eurico's former translator said he still kept in touch with his wife, who came from the family of a revered independence fighter slain by the Indonesians. 'She keeps on asking me for money, but I can't give her as much now since I have taken on another wife and she is costing a lot of money,' he beamed. 'The next time you're in Timor-Leste, you should be sure to look her up.' I did, and she seemed to bear him no ill-will, either. He still sends money to his cousins in his hometown to help pay for ceremonies.

Once again, it seemed that friendships, family ties, and old allegiances were stronger than any indictment could be, and that moral absolutes were almost entirely absent. There are human discrepancies between international covenants on human rights and the reality of how people get along in a small society. I went to West Timor naïvely imagining that, somehow, those connections between the Timorese on either side of the border had been severed. It turned out that I had totally underestimated how ties persisted, no matter what. It seemed that nothing done in this small society could permanently estrange anyone. It's almost as if many of the Timorese elite have got 1999 out of their system better than the international community has, and that, for the locals, the period is marked down as an especially turbulent chapter — but no more than that — in Timor's history. Eurico's cousins still send their children to stay in his house when they study in Kupang. Life is both simpler and much more complicated than a Security Council mandate.

A Finland–Soviet Union complex also drives engagement between Timor-Leste and its larger neighbour. Pursuing good ties with Indonesia seems an objective of almost every leading Timorese politician. The past seems remarkably uncontroversial. The push to forgive and forget is led by the senior political leadership, which responds to the violence of history as a matter requiring pragmatism and reconciliation, and not criminal sanctions. The argument seems to be that wounds can only heal if they are closed over. His comrade Xanana Gusmao — a man captured and jailed by the Indonesians — has publicly hugged some of the generals who once spent years trying to capture or kill him. When he visits Bali, where his brother is a senior figure in customs at the airport, Xanana stays in the hotel that is run by one of his ex-jailers.

A faded photo of Xanana on the day of his capture in Dili in 1992 hung proudly in Joanico Cesario Belo's house on the day that I went to visit him just outside Kupang. The picture had discoloured badly over time — the distinctive blood-red berets of the three Indonesian elite soldiers pictured with their arms around their prize capture had faded to a weak shade of orange.

An old man and woman in black clothes (which indicated that they were in a period of mourning) shuffled into one of the dark corners of the room. As he talked, they kept looking back and forth between the photograph and me as Joanico told me he was ready to return to Dili to face a court should any charges be brought against him. In 1999, he had been the commander of Tim Saka, an Indonesian army unit stationed in Baucau. He was later credited by human-rights observers as having had a moderating influence on the troops under his command. In the early 1990s, he was a UN military observer in Bosnia–Herzegovina, Cambodia, and Rwanda; he told me he was one of the last officers to leave before the genocide in the central African nation.

Suddenly, he changed conversational gears. 'So who do you recognise in that photo?' he asked. Xanana, of course, but there had to be someone else that I knew, I thought, as I went to peer at the washed-out print. I looked at the other three men, trying to figure out what any of them might look like twenty years later. How many elite Indonesian soldiers did I know? Suddenly, I had an epiphany. 'You!' I said, pointing to Joanico. The years had treated Joanico well and, apart from his hair being a bit shorter, he really didn't look that much different. He smiled, and the old couple laughed. Joanico said he was one of the men who had discovered where Xanana Gusmao had been hiding out and who had planned his capture. The guerrilla leader had come down from the mountains and had been hiding in a small bunker built underneath the house of one of his relatives in Dili. He'd come to the city to help oversee the transfer of an arms shipment and to conduct meetings with members of the clandestine movement. An informer who had seen Xanana sneak out one night for an assignation had told the Indonesians, and Joanico lay in a hillock overlooking the house to vouch for the information.

Emblematic of the topsy-turvy hall of mirrors that is Timorese politics, the two men still keep in touch. His one-time captor travels to Bali to see Xanana every time the Timorese leader is passing through. 'He asks me for strategic and military advice, and sometimes sends ministers down to my house to seek counsel.' Joanico told me this as if it was the most natural thing in the world. He said they were good friends.

Like everything on this journey, one meeting was leading to another; one relationship opening up another encounter. I asked Joanico about the Timorese who were living outside of Kupang in refugee settlements, and he said that it would be much better if I went to see for myself, rather than listening to him. He gave me the number of Francisco Ximenes, a leader in one of the camps. 'Go talk to him,' he said, 'and he will tell you how we are suffering.' The old couple nodded.

Francisco was known to be a wise man. He lived about an hour outside of Kupang on the road to Atambua and near the centre of the camp that housed about 5,000 people; at one point just after the referendum vote, nearly twenty times that number were there. I had imagined somehow that, by definition, a camp meant that people would be living in tents. Instead, the inhabitants were living in thatched huts that didn't look very different from many of the houses they would have lived in on the other side of the border. The residents were dressed in a series of odd Western cast-offs. We got lost, and an old woman who directed us to Francisco's house was wearing a T-shirt the wrong way round, which meant that a picture of David Beckham was across her back. An 'Operation Iraqi Freedom' beach towel was drying on the line. Other apparel was less benign — we saw an old man carrying a pail of water wearing a brown T-shirt bearing the name of Eurico's militia.

Francisco seemed glad to see me, and my arrival was clearly the most interesting thing that had happened to him in months. He was in his early sixties, with a barrelled belly that he said he'd acquired following his retirement from the Indonesian army; he was now living on his pension. I remarked that his face looked familiar, and he said that people told him that he looked like his cousin, a pro-independence fighter who was now a member of parliament. At every turn, I seemed to be uncovering unlikely linkages.

He and the rest of his camp-dwellers seemed to be in stasis. Some resettlement houses had been built for families, but he said that they were much too small for even a few people, never mind the sprawling Timorese arrangements. (I counted at least fifteen people wandering in and out of his house during the hour we spent with him.) The new homes were far away from land to till, but it seemed that people preferred to stay put, living a 'neither-here-nor-there' sort of existence on land owned by the Indonesian military.

The people in the camp certainly felt very much like the

forgotten people that Meno Hornay had talked about, scratching out an existence far away even from Kupang itself. I asked Francisco why many people didn't want to return and seemed happy to eke things out over the border in West Timor. Some, like him, had pensions, he told me, which they could only receive if they resided in Indonesia, but many were apprehensive about what might happen to them if they went back. They'd heard of returnees being slighted, insulted, and killed — each incident no doubt amplified by the always-febrile Timorese rumour mill. 'We are scared,' he said simply. Behind the patina of reconciliation and familial friendship, neighbour still feared neighbour. On the other side of the border, too, it seemed that although the leaders might have moved on to a different chapter, this did not necessarily apply to of their followers.

We pushed on up the road to Atambua, another one of those towns that people are only likely to have heard of because something bad once happened there. This town of wide boulevards would be known to most people outside the island of Timor primarily for an attack in 2000 when three United Nations staff were murdered by a pro-autonomy militia that ran amok following the death of their leader. Just thirty kilometres from the border, Atambua was one of the main centres for Timorese who fled the violence; the UN staff members were working on refugee return when they were attacked. Their bodies were dragged from the office out onto the street and burnt. Other UN staff survived only by jumping from the high barbed-wired walls that were meant to protect them.

I'd avoided the town on my previous short forays in and out of West Timor. There was something about the name of the place that gave me the creeps, and I always drove with the car windows up between Oecusse and the border, without passing through Atambua. My Timorese colleagues had the opposite reaction; they seemed to value a workshop or meeting in Oecusse, as much for the opportunity to spend the night in Atambua and to go shopping the following day as they did for visiting the enclave. Staples and consumer goods were much cheaper on this side of the border, and, as we drove into town, we noticed that a significant number of cars parked in town had Timor-Leste registration plates. One garish white hotel that looked as if Imelda Marcos had designed it was apparently built with visiting Timor-Leste government dignitaries and officials in mind, who arrived laden with generous *per diem* allowances.

Our lodgings was significantly less up-market; the VIP rooms we were staying in cost just US$10 a night. The hotel was run by an elderly Indonesian–Chinese family who had spent most of the occupation in Dili working in the hospital. The wife spoke good Tetun, and she told me she felt honoured that Eurico and his entourage had recently chosen her lodgings over other options. 'In fact, you are sleeping where Eurico sleeps,' she told me proudly. With eyes fluttering like a love-struck teenager, one of the guards described him as a good man popular with the ladies. As my bed squeaked ominously that night, I really wished he hadn't told me this fact.

Atambua was a staging post on the final part of this journey: a meeting with Maternus Bere, the infamous former militia commander who vies with Eurico as the most notorious of all the pro-Indonesian men of 1999. His infamy comes not just because of the severity of the charges against him but because, in 2009, he was caught and subsequently released by Timorese authorities, allegedly under pressure from the government of Indonesia.

As noted earlier, there are over four hundred Timorese indicted for serious crimes that took place in the run-up to and the aftermath of the vote for independence. Many of them are living in plain sight in Indonesia, and most are just over the border in

West Timor. The problem of what to do with former leaders such as Maternus Bere is something that both governments prefer to keep in the background. With Bere's arrest, the matter became front-page news; the drama played out with world attention on the country, as it coincided with the tenth anniversary of the vote for independence. The decision to free Bere prompted outrage from opposition parties, civil society, and human-rights NGOs. It even drew an unusually direct reproach from the normally anxious-not-to-offend United Nations mission, who accused the Timorese government of trading victims' rights for peaceable relations. The justice minister justified the decision in terms of the national interest. The prime minister acknowledged that, although the transfer of Bere was technically illegal under Timorese law, his tiny country could not afford to provoke its larger neighbour, as it was still dependent upon it for, among other things, food and petrol. Despite the reserves in the Timor Sea, all the fuel that fills the cars in Dili is Indonesian. Most of it is supplied by the Indonesian state oil company, a durable and commercial success-story that operates out of the same facilities it built during the occupation, and whose depot provided the fuel to burn Dili down in 1999. Timor-Leste is so small that Indonesia could put it in its pocket. The country is independent, but still very much dependent on Indonesia.

After Bere's repatriation, the man himself faded back into obscurity, so it took no end of phone calls and connections for me to track him down. He lived in the mountains near the south coast, just on the Indonesian side of the border, another five hours from Atambua along steadily deteriorating roads.

As we clattered along, my translator said she could not believe that such abominable road conditions still existed in her country. She had never been this far in West Timor, and couldn't believe what she was seeing. 'Corruption,' explained Anato, our fixer, who had arranged the meeting. 'The companies get the contracts, but then they don't buy proper asphalt and, even then, they only coat half the road with half the required thickness. It's a big problem.' Our phones beeped in unison. It was Timor Telecom welcoming us to Timor-Leste; we were so close to the frontier that our mobiles roamed onto the nearby country's network.

My companions started speaking Indonesian to each other, and my mind turned to the man I was going to meet, a former civil servant and school teacher accused of extermination, murder, enforced disappearance, rape, torture, and a catalogue of other inhuman acts. One of the most infamous acts of which he stands accused was of participating in the firebombing and strafing of a church in which hundreds of Timorese had sought refuge from his militia. Indonesian police and military officers had also allegedly participated, and up to two hundred people had died. His 63-page indictment by the United Nations Special Panel on Serious Crimes reads like the plot of a horror movie. I've never been able to get through the whole document in one go.

As we bumped along the track, I wondered what this man would look like now and how he would act. A picture of him taken during the militia rampages showed a man with long, black hair and a flowing beard that made him look like a vengeful prophet.

Just when I thought that this journey would never end, we turned into a glade with two wooden dwellings that reminded me of the setting for a Grimm's fairy tale. The man who came out of one of the houses did not look like his picture. Clean-shaven, with a standard-length barbered haircut, Bere was dressed in the Sunday best that he had worn to mass that morning. He spoke more like a kindly uncle than someone indicted for crimes against humanity.

He was happy to talk, and many members of his extended family gathered around him while Anato went off to check if there were any Indonesian intelligence officers lurking at the back of the house to eavesdrop on our conversation. When he returned, he gave me the thumbs up and we began. I started by asking Bere what had happened in 2009.

He answered in an unexpected way, beginning in the fifteenth century, long before the arrival of the Portuguese and the Dutch, when almost the entire island was united under the kingdom of Wehali. Many of the Timorese integrationists used the example of Wehali to substantiate their reasoning that the island should be under one ruler. On the way down to Maternus' house, we had visited the remnants of this once-great and all-powerful kingdom that once stretched across most of the island and seemed now, to the naked eye, little more than a few ramshackle homes and spirit houses along the side of a road. In Maternus' mind's eye, this impression of long-faded glory was totally mistaken: the woes of the eastern part of the island in which he lived were due to a still-potent curse handed down by the kingdom of Wehali over the kingdom of Maubara all those years ago. What had happened in 1999 was just the latest in a long series of calamities that went back hundreds of years. He wrote down the curse in my notebook and said that I should not incant the words out loud lest I fall foul of it myself. As I was quickly realising, Bere and his family lived at the edge of a supernatural and spiritual world where the distant past had not yet passed but was still mingled with the present. The story of the curse was part of the same narrative five hundred years later. In Bere's world, accusations laid down in dry legal English by curiously robed lawyers who were versed in the complexities of international justice and Security Council mandates were as other-worldly as the lawyers would have found his stories about men who effortlessly harnessed the spirits of past generations.

Bere talked for hours — twenty minutes was taken up with a

story about a mystic griffin — and no amount of gentle interjection could direct him back to the topics I had really come to talk about. The conversation was a treasure trove for an anthropologist; but, with night drawing in, he still hadn't even touched on his arrest and his propulsion to the status of international cause célèbre. It was getting dark, and our driver's fidgeting conveyed his anxiousness about the long road back. Sensing that, at this pace, we could be here until morning, Anato slipped him a note asking him to fast-forward. He sighed. We clearly had no appreciation of the past. But he reluctantly agreed, and started to talk about 5 August 2009, the day he crossed the border back into Timor-Leste, for the first time in ten years. He said he had decided to return in order to attend a religious ceremony for his godson. He had travelled on his Indonesian passport, and at the crossing point, known as Salt River, Timorese immigration authorities had issued him with a tourist visa as if he had been any other visitor. UN police advisers to the Timorese border police lingering around had appeared not to notice anything untoward. The taxi drivers who waited to overcharge unwary new arrivals for the ride into town had waved to acknowledge him.

He spent three days in the town of Suai, and lost track of how many people met him in the street and hugged him. When he went to Sunday mass, he said that the choir changed the words of the hymns so they sounded like cantos of forgiveness. When he told me this, he broke down and cried.

He was arrested a day later, and says that neither he nor the public defender or court officials — all, according to him, former students from his days as a schoolteacher — could understand why. Bere acknowledges that he was a senior figure in the militia in the border town of Suai during 1999, but nothing more. His involvement, he said, had extended to no more than spirited advocacy for Timor remaining a part of Indonesia. He knew nothing about any violence after the ballot, when militias ran amok — a claim that some might find a little hard to credit in a tightly knit society in which nothing is a secret for too long.

The Timorese police certainly seemed to have taken him at his word. The officer who drove him to Dili said there was no need for handcuffs, as he was a 'good and well-respected man'. He spent a few weeks in the main jail, and has fond memories of playing volleyball with fellow prisoners — among them, those accused of attempting to assassinate the president in 2008. (I later asked the petitioner leader, Gastao Salsinha, about Bere, and he remembered him as an agile sportsman.)

Bere attended mass daily. 'You were praying for divine intervention?' I ventured, thinking that I'd have been in an almighty panic had I been arrested for crimes against humanity and had my jailers been the cousins of people I had allegedly killed. 'Not at all,' he answered, a bit perplexed by my peculiar thought-process. 'I had been forgiven a few years ago.' His trial did not take place in a court, but in the course of a terrifying dream which, he says, was much more important, as it was probably sanctified by a higher authority.

In his dream state, he'd soared over the peaks of the steep mountains and bounded back into Suai, the town he'd purportedly laid to waste. He was caught — he can't remember how — and was strapped onto an altar with an Indonesian flag behind him as a baying throng from his home town decided his fate. He could remember their screams, and he thought that this was what Jesus must have felt like when the crowds decided his fate. A priest with long hair and dried blood on his hands ran the tip of a sword over and over his stomach, and stood ready to plunge the blade into his heart, but the people changed their minds and then beseeched that he be spared. He woke up covered in sweat, but knew the slate had been wiped clean. 'I had been absolved and redeemed,' he said. He subsequently made a confession to a priest and — according to the laws of the Catholic Church — he was now forgiven. His cousin had been listening as he spoke and nodded solemnly that this was so. If God forgave him, then he could have no fear of a court. He said that he presumed that, as a fellow Catholic, I must understand.

On the morning of 30 August 2009 — the ten-year anniversary of the vote that his militia had so vehemently opposed — he was on his way to morning mass when the prison guards told him there had been a change of plan. The president had ordered his transfer to the Indonesian embassy in Dili. The Indonesian foreign minister had flown as far as Kupang, but refused to fly onto Dili to attend the ceremonies marking the occasion without citizen Bere being moved into the embassy. This delayed the start of the ceremony by hours, and the governor-general of Australia was obliged to kick her heels in the airport when Timorese officials refused to tell her what was going on. What did the governor-general, a former member of the Australian Human Rights Commission, make of this? Adherence to protocol meant she was too polite to say. But it was clear that Timor-Leste was much more scared of one near neighbour than the other. It knew what Indonesia was capable of.

Bere spent two months there, reading books and watching television, before he was spirited out of the country in the dead of night, on the probably specious grounds that he needed urgent medical treatment. He looked the picture of health these days and, as he bid us farewell, he told me to come back soon. He said he had many more stories still to tell.

Chapter Six

A Land of Babel

No one knows for sure, but there are estimated to be at least twenty identifiably different languages spoken in this country, which is half the size of Tasmania.

I began Chapter One of this book in a region called Oecusse. They speak Baikeno there, a language completely unintelligible to anyone from any other part of the country. The Oecusse police commander, who hails from Ainaro, says that it took him years to master it; I remember him telling me that it was harder than English. The commander's mother tongue is Mambai, the language that the anthropologist Elizabeth Traube characterised as sometimes used in a way that cloaked rather than revealed the speaker's thoughts. Mambai is also the mother tongue of Fernando 'La Sama' de Araujo, the former president of the parliament and now vice prime minister. The journalist Jose Belo is one of the few thousand people in the world who speaks Wa'ima, a language restricted to a pocket of the northern coast near the city of Baucau, and the object of particular fascination among linguists for its tonal characteristics.

When Jose was growing up, he heard both that language and Makassae, which means he speaks it fluently, too, and he used this language to communicate with the FALINTIL hiding out in the mountains and jungles in the east. Makassae is tonal and structurally different from the other languages around it, so members of the resistance used it as a secret lingo to out-fox the Indonesians and also to ensure that what was being said wasn't understood by fellow Timorese, whom they did not necessarily trust, from other regions. When Jose wants to talk about a sensitive issue with Taur Matan Ruak, he can, if he wants to, switch to Makassae. Like many Timorese, they switch between three or four languages with ease.

The use of regional languages helped stoke the grievances of the petitioning soldiers in 2006. They felt excluded because the people from the east spoke to them in languages that they could not understand. The mother tongue of their leader, Gastao Salsinha, is Kemak, a language spoken by about 100,000 people in the damp hills in western Timor-Leste and across the border in Indonesia. In each of the thirteen districts, the people speak one and sometimes two or more additional tongues. The Chinese community in Timor speak their own language called Hakka, the language of the Chinese region of their ancestors.

A linguistic map of the country is multi-coloured and multi-speckled, and even more varied after the arrival of the large-scale international presence in the late-1990s. Portuguese is the language of the law and the courts, but the majority of embassies and international organisations use English as a way to communicate — a strategy that has had mixed success. English is the default language on restaurant menus, but the Indonesian language remains commonly heard. Indonesia is, by far, Timor-Leste's largest trading partner, and the provider of the soap operas beamed into Timorese homes each night. For many viewers watching out in the districts, the jaunty commercials in Indonesian that they see for toothpaste, soap powder, and household essentials are windows onto another world.

The newly minted Timorese business elite and the international advisers now share the smoky lobby of the Hotel Timor, but the restaurant remains forever a bit of Portugal. As an English friend of mine said, it reminded him of the cavernous eating halls his parents took him to during childhood holidays at the Algarve. Starched linen covers the tables, and Portuguese-speaking Timorese waitstaff sashay from table to table ferrying meat and potato-based dishes, with barely a lettuce leaf in sight — salad is as atypical as an empty ashtray. I couldn't get enough of the place, no matter how challenging some of the chef's recipes were. I credit a combination of the octopus and bean stew, followed by a double brandy, with having once staved off a heavy cold that was about to engulf me.

In the restaurant, I talked with some Portuguese teachers about their efforts to introduce their mother tongue into Timorese schools. The country's education policy stipulates that Portuguese be taught as the language of instruction in schools, but there is a problem: most Timorese teachers have limited capabilities in the language, or none at all. Estimates vary, but no more than 10–15 per cent of Timorese have basic proficiency in Portuguese. Hence, it's back to school for the teachers. Portugal sends hundreds of language instructors each year to Timor-Leste to teach the teachers.

With some exceptions, the Timorese teachers are proving to be less than A-grade students. Many of the older teachers have long lost whatever Portuguese they may have learned at school. Many have not studied the language for years, and find the grammar, tenses, and prepositions complicated; most of them don't do their homework. The problem is even worse for the younger ones. The language was banned during Indonesian times, so they have no familiarity with it at all. Other problems transcend the age gap. No matter what age they are, many plainly lack sufficient interest, or perhaps are simply too tired from their teaching work and familial obligations, to invest the time necessary to learn a new language. Others are actively resentful about having to learn what they believe is not a useful language. Portugal is a far-away cousin and not necessarily a popular one; not all Timorese look back on the Portuguese era with fondness. Whether because of a lack of interest or a shortage of people with whom to practise the language, the majority find Portuguese to be extremely difficult. They switch off the Portuguese-language bulletin that follows the Tetun edition of the evening news, and instead click to the hammy Javanese melodramas on the satellite.

When the teachers move back to their classrooms, the thin results of all this expensive effort are plain to see. The teachers hesitantly start their classes in Portuguese and look tense, feeling self-conscious at the sound of the words coming from their mouths. They make simple errors and tell their students off for their 'mistakes', even when they are not making them. Confusion reigns until the teachers slowly slip back into Tetun. I can sympathise. I myself tried learning Portuguese in Dili and, although we had a wonderful teacher called Sandra, my efforts petered out because the only place I could really practise the language was in the Hotel Timor restaurant. When the waiters couldn't understand my pronunciation, I switched to Tetun. 'Speak Tetun, it's much easier to understand, *malae*,' one of them said to me one day. The efforts to reintroduce Portuguese after a lapse of a quarter-century are taking place in an extremely unpropitious laboratory.

The Portuguese instructors — many of whom haven't made much of an effort to learn Tetun, the national *lingua franca*, to say nothing of the local languages — are puzzled that the Timorese teachers don't want to learn their language, and they also feel under pressure to demonstrate success. The language-instruction program is costing the cash-strapped Portuguese government a lot of money. Bureaucrats managing the aid program do not want to hear dappled socio-cultural explanations about why so many Timorese are failing their exams: they want fast results to report to their masters in Lisbon. Reporting success in the program requires thick slathers of spin.

Somewhat ironically, Portugal is giving much more priority to language development now than it did when it governed the country. During the Portuguese period, the large majority of Timorese children did not even attend elementary school — education was a privilege extended only to the families of the Timorese elite, or to those who worked in the colonial administration. It does not sound as though it was a lot of fun. According to memoirs, the style of instruction in the colonial classroom was frequently cold and brutal. Teachers would mock the students for speaking anything other than Portuguese, and there are accounts of teachers slapping and punching the young learners when they spoke Tetun — which, although or perhaps because it contained a lot of Portuguese words, was considered to be an inferior pidgin.

In fact, Tetun is not the child-like pidgin that some claim it to be, but is a language in its own right; it predates Portuguese by many centuries, and it originated not far from where Maternus Bere now lives. Tetun (which the Portuguese spell as 'Tetum') is the language of Wehali, the once-powerful ritual centre of the island. The Wehali considered themselves akin to a ruling class. According to their legends, their region was the first to come out of the sea; as the oldest part of the island, they thought themselves pre-eminent over other areas, and their language of higher importance than the other tongues. (In other words, the Tetun speakers looked down on the other languages in the way that Portuguese speakers looked down on Tetun.)

It is believed that, before the arrival of the Portuguese and Dutch colonists, the influence and power of the Wehali lords extended far beyond their lands on the south coast, reaching from Oecusse and Baucau in the north to the tar sands of Viqueque in the south. Hierarchy dictated that, in order to communicate with the *liurai* from Wehali, people had to learn their language, Tetun, and, during this process, Tetun began to filter into other languages for words such as those for parts of the body, crops, and geographical features. Tetun became the *lingua franca* that Timorese from different areas used to communicate with each other when they didn't understand each other's local languages. (Tellingly, Tetun words can be found in all languages in Timor-Leste.) The remnants of the kingdom today can be found in West Timor, halfway between Atambua and Maternus Bere's house.

The Portuguese crushed the kingdom of Wehali but co-opted their language, which had spread through elite marriage. So it was that, being the language in most common usage, Tetun became the bridging language between the representatives of the Portuguese crown and the kingdoms of Timor. Rather than going out to the hills, the Portuguese summoned the kings to Dili to confirm their loyalty; Tetun became the language by which all these leaders from various parts of Timor used to communicate with each other, using the ritual language of Wehali supplemented with borrowed words from the Portuguese language they heard around them. In order to shore up their rule, the Portuguese sealed alliances with the local *liurai*; accordingly, ceremonial words such as *documentos* for documents and *carimbu* for the waxed stamps that sealed these baroque certificates entered the lexicon.

Tetun words began to be mixed with a new vocabulary that contained words for items and concepts which had not previously existed on the island. The newcomers from across the seas wore trousers and shirts and shoes on their feet, the words for which had had no reason to exist in Tetun because the Timorese did not wear these items. The Portuguese terms were duly adopted, as were the Portuguese names for the new fruits and vegetables that they brought to the island. This meant that, nearly five hundred years later, people in both Ainaro and the Algarve use the same word for items such as 'apple' and 'pumpkin'.

A similar process of linguistic amalgamation, combination, and adaption happened in religion. The Wehali called their god *Maromak*, and the missionaries kept the word but refashioned the meaning. In Portuguese–Tetun dictionaries and catechisms, the priests spread the word of *Aman Maromak*, God the Father, the Christian God, and told the Timorese something they had not heard before: Maromak had a son, called Jesus. Tetun words were used in the Christian liturgy, Catholicism, and animism, happily co-existing and co-mingling with each other.

In four hundred of years of colonialism, Portuguese never came close to being the majority language in Timor (nor did Catholicism become the dominant religion). As with English in the former colonies of the British Empire, Portuguese was the language that the local elite used to communicate with their vassals. Although many Timorese knew a fair number of Portuguese words, most people could not string them together into sentences. The Portuguese-speaking revolutionaries, themselves the children of the elite, were among the small percentage of the population who had attained complete fluency in the language. That was why, when a Portuguese TV crew came to Timor to cover the civil war and set off for the hills to meet with the armed groups, they encountered an unexpected problem: almost none of the men the camera pointed at could utter anything more than a few pleasantries in Portuguese. The presenter had to keep returning to the same person for comment — a bushy-haired commander called Rogerio Lobato.

The young revolutionaries of 1975 were afflicted by the same complicated relationship with the capital as were those who had agitated for independence in other colonies. At one level, they were deeply influenced by the Euro-Atlantic culture, ideas, and literature that they had learned in school; but, on the other hand, Portuguese denigration of their own national languages helped fire them up to demand that the island become a territory independent from Portugal. Language was a crucial signifier of difference. The FRETILIN party turned *maubere*, a Mambai word used by the Portuguese as a shorthand phrase for 'stupid and ignorant', into a proudly patriotic term referring to 'the people', signifying difference and national self-confidence. (Jose Ramos-Horta and Anna Pessoa named their son Lorosa'e Maubere.)

This curate's egg of love and loathing was reflected in the political platform of the nine-day republic in 1975. When the Democratic Republic of Timor-Leste was proclaimed, the constitution stated that the official language would be Portuguese; this became an article of faith throughout the long years of Indonesian occupation, re-affirmed time and again at national conventions in exile. The Portuguese phrase *a luta continua* ('the struggle continues') became the slogan of the resistance, and mottos in Portuguese were invoked as a means to demonstrate that Timor was a different country from that of the Malay-speaking Indonesian invaders. Members of the resistance, educated in colonial times, used Portuguese as a secret language for writing documents, reports, and letters that only they could read, and bestowed Portuguese names on tasks and positions. Jose Belo and Gastao Salsinha were among those known by the Portuguese word *estafeta*, meaning 'messenger'; their job was to take communications written on small scraps of paper from one commander to another. Often, it was too dangerous to carry the message on their person, so the *estafetas* hid the messages in an array of everyday items. One of Jose's ruses was to wrap the message in the plastic film that comes with a fresh packet of cigarettes, hollow out a pumpkin, slip the note inside, and then set the vegetable amid a pile of others.

Portuguese had profound symbolic value, but it was not used in everyday life. As a result, many of the younger generation of *estafetas* may know what a word means, but cannot (and could not then) form sentences with the word in it. The Indonesians prohibited the use of Portuguese, and castigated the language as a colonial remnant. Any Timorese who were heard speaking Portuguese risked a jail sentence, as the new occupiers aggressively went about putting their Indonesian stamp on the territory, renaming the province *Timor Timur*. The process began in schools. In 1974, the few Timorese who went to school were taught, in Portuguese, the names of the rivers running through Lisbon and Porto; a few years later, the same students were learning the state ideology of Indonesia in the Indonesian language. No longer would education be the preserve of a small minority. Education was expanded, and schools were built in each hamlet of the country as part of a campaign to win the population over.

The process continued in the civil service. The language changed, but the reputation of the civil service for torpidity and inertia remained, prompting the gloriously alliterative Indonesian phrase *datang, duduk, diam, duit*, which translates as 'arrive, sit down, shut up, and get paid'. (One could claim bureaucratic sloth was a form of passive resistance but, ten years after independence, the same pattern of 'arriving late and leaving early' continues for many, occasionally prompting splenetic outbursts from the prime minister.) Indonesian was necessary to talk to the occupiers, but it was also a means of getting access to opportunities. Even FALINTIL fighters high in the mountains learned it. I heard a story that, on one occasion, they chose not to kill a captured soldier, and instead used him as their in-camp language instructor. He must have been an extremely good teacher — footage taken in the late-1990s shows the FALINTIL fighters baiting enemy soldiers over a radio, using fluent Indonesian slang.

The only place where Indonesian was not spoken was inside a church. With Portuguese banned, Tetun became the new language of the liturgy. In a way that it had not been during Portuguese times, Catholicism came to symbolise a form of collective identity that was culturally different from predominantly Muslim Indonesians. The church was the only place in which Timorese could gather *en masse* without risking arrest; Catholicism thereby became a symbol of opposition to the Indonesian occupation, and Tetun a potent symbol of Timorese separateness. Before the Indonesian invasion, the number of Catholics was estimated to have been just about one-quarter of the population; now, nearly all Timorese identify themselves as Catholic.

The linguistic shift within occupied Timor went largely unnoticed because the island was so remote. The Timorese political elite who lived abroad — mainly in Lisbon, Maputo, and Macau — used Portuguese as their language of communication, assuming that the same would naturally have happened back home. But it was not so. When the former leaders who left in 1975 returned nearly a quarter of a century later, they found a linguistically changed country. Portuguese was spoken by a minority of the older generation, but many of the youth spoke Indonesian more comfortably; and many seemed more interested in learning English — the language of the United Nations administration and donors, and hence a potential source of employment — than the language of the old colony. But the language used most commonly of all was Tetun. It was the language of the street, the playground, the text message, the radio, and the newspapers — although, to confuse matters, Tetun numerals tend only to be used to describe numbers of people. Portuguese or Indonesian numerals are still used to describe numbers of items or when swapping phone numbers.

The question of what was to be the national language was among the big, initial questions for the state's new leaders to answer. In numeric terms, either Tetun or Indonesian would have been the most widely spoken tongue, but the problem was much more complicated and loaded than the simple matter of what language people chose to speak. The question came freighted with issues of national identity, and was bound up with looming decisions about which direction — if any — the country would tilt towards diplomatically, and where the new state would fit in with the rest of the world. Would it adopt Indonesian, the language of the country that surrounded it, which would be its biggest trading partner, and which had left behind practices and marks such as uniforms, administrative forms, toy-town official badges, and, most especially, cuisine? What about Portuguese, the language of the old colony, thousands of miles away, which had bequeathed its architecture, religion, law, hierarchies, and titles so deeply that sometimes it felt as though it had never left? Some suggested English, the global *lingua franca* spoken as a mother tongue in the country to the south, and where some young adults had been educated when their parents fled with them in 1975. Or should it be Tetun, a language spoken by the majority, but which both its detractors and proponents agreed needed development and standardisation? The debate took place largely among the Lusophone-inflected elite, which may explain the result.

According to the solution adopted in the constitution, Timor-Leste has two official languages: Tetun and Portuguese. In addition, there are two 'working languages', which are English and Indonesian, and the constitution also notes the special status of all the other languages spoken in the territory. The constitution has a heavy Portuguese flavour, and scholars have also detected a close resemblance between it and the constitution of the old colonial power. Perhaps this is not so surprising, given that Anna Pessoa Pinto, Jose Ramos-Horta's former wife, the previous hostage of Rogerio Lobato and a judge in Mozambique, drafted the 'working text' of the constitution. She was then a non-Tetun speaker (although she now speaks it flawlessly). I once heard that she hadn't accommodated the arguments submitted at the time that weren't in Portuguese because she couldn't understand them.

Having a quadri-lingual constitution is unusual, but not unique. Many European and Asian countries have two or more official languages. Some countries, such as South Africa and India, have two digits worth of official languages — eleven and twenty-two respectively. The problem in Timor-Leste is not the number of languages *per se*, but the fact that government documents are not translated, creating the crazy situation whereby official laws and policies go over the heads of those who are meant to enact or implement them. The leaders from the 1975 generation can read the laws, but few of those who cut their teeth during the Indonesian period can read Portuguese to the standard required. Legislation is drafted in Portuguese and is not translated into Tetun as a matter of course, which means that the majority of parliamentarians debate and vote on laws that they can't read; in turn, government departments implement legislation that they don't understand. Compounding the problem is the fact that most of the Portuguese lawyers drafting the legislation, whose Tetun language skills were no better than those of the visiting teachers, meant that the laws were written devoid of Timorese context. One of the results of this situation is that, on the

Portuguese evening-news bulletins, whenever parliamentarians are asked to comment on a political development, the same handful of MPs is always turned to: they are the only ones who feel comfortable speaking the language on television.

No wonder the law often appears so poorly enforced, when those charged with implementing it do not understand it. Until Nelson Belo's NGO received a grant to translate the security laws, the police and military were meant to be enforcing a set of laws that they literally could not read. When my old research assistant Julio, now Secretary of State for Defence, launched the translations, he said that, for the first time, he would now have a completely accurate understanding of the laws that crossed his desk.

Some influential Timorese argue that, far from bringing quadrilingual fluency, allowing so many languages to be used just creates four times the level of confusion.

Perhaps the biggest problem is that the language used the most is developed the least. Mocked by the Portuguese, and denigrated by the Indonesians, the development of Tetun as a written language for daily use still remains relatively neglected, even since independence. Even though there is now a standardised Tetun orthography, its use is the exception rather than the rule, and there are no standard practices in translation and interpreting. Different spellings and usage conventions turn publications into a jarring pastiche of personal styles. Newspapers use any old spelling, which benefits learners like me — in that one can spell a word about ten different ways and still not necessarily be wrong — but it wreaks havoc for standardisation of the written language. Complicating the embedding of the language still further is the fact that, according to Save the Children, over 50 per cent of Timorese are illiterate.

Successive governments' rhetorical commitment to the development of Tetun as a national language has not been matched in either budgetary support or human sweat. Many civil servants can neither read nor write Tetun to a comprehensible standard. The National Institute of Linguistics, charged with promoting the language, receives a stipend of just US$6,000 a year, and its offices are two poky rooms that were locked every time I tried to visit them.

The institute seems in deep-freeze. Donors prepared a plan to invigorate it, but it did not go ahead, allegedly because the relevant individuals did not have the time to sign off on the proposal. The institute today is an even more forlorn place than the offices of the Truth and Reconciliation Commission and, like CAVR, it is hard to believe that it was also once a place of great energy. In the space of a few years in the middle of the last decade, the institute produced a flurry of dictionaries in Tetun, Baikeno, and Fataluku, grammar guides, orthographies, and even its own in-house academic journal. The driving force behind the institute seemed to be an Australian linguist called Geoffrey Hull, and his name was on the cover of many of the books that they produced. (White Bat had told me he'd found one of his books a surprisingly comfortable pillow.) The rapid decline from an engine-room of learning to a few bolted rooms was inexplicable. What had happened?

I thought finding the answer would be easy — I'd just go and find Geoffrey Hull, and ask him. But, even in a world made accessible by Google, this proved extremely difficult. According to a web-search, he was affiliated to two universities in Sydney; yet, when I rang up the relevant departments, they said there was no one of that name there. I couldn't find an obituary, so I assumed that he was still alive. But he seemed to have disappeared off the map. No one in Dili knew how to find him, either, and I was out of ideas as to what to try next.

Then, out of the blue, the man himself got in touch with me about a month later. He had retired prematurely, 'partly from burnout in Timor', but he still lived in the Sydney area, and had an honorary affiliation in the ancient history department at Macquarie University. I sent him the synopsis of this book, and he said he'd been happy to meet me. He'd been asked to comment many times before about his experiences in Timor, but had chosen not to do so; since I was from Northern Ireland, he'd make an exception.

He greeted me warmly in the Ulster dialect of Irish Gaelic, one of the tens of languages he speaks. I had learned the language at school, but couldn't speak it; in percentage terms, fewer speak this official language of Ireland than speak Portuguese in Timor-Leste. We went for a coffee, and decided that it would probably be easier if we spoke English.

The professor had become interested in Timor during the late 1980s, when he had worked as an occasional translator for various Australian government departments. Among his clients at the time were Portuguese-speaking Timorese who had fled to Australia in 1975, and his interest in the languages of the island went from there. He said that he had felt some natural solidarity with them, given they shared the same Catholic faith. They had given him a copy of St Mark's Gospel in Tetun, and also an old Portuguese–Tetun dictionary prepared at the turn of the century, and he had begun to familiarise himself with this new language. He told me that he could speak it after a couple of weeks — somehow, he managed to make this incredible statement in a matter-of-fact way that sounded humble, not arrogant — and he had begun to work on a handbook for foreigners who wanted to learn Tetun. Shortly after the independence vote, Ramos-Horta had asked him to come to Dili to provide intellectual heft to the new institute by helping to codify and standardise a language in which some speakers mixed Portuguese words; others, Indonesian; and still others, expressions from their native languages.

It was an intellectual challenge of the highest order, but one that he seemed to approach with relish. He set out how verbs and nouns functioned, worked out a system of spelling, and determined sounds. His dictionaries reflected his belief that Tetun was a 'Europeanised' Austronesian language influenced heavily by four hundred years of Portuguese. Spelling included diacritic marks ('accents' to the non-linguist) above some letters, and its higher or more advanced vocabulary borrowed heavily from Portuguese. He seemed to pump out these books with accomplished ease.

It wasn't complex linguistic rules that would bring him down, but the multifarious and frequently intensely personal politics around him. By his own account, the institute was an even more claustrophobic font of jealousies, hurt pride, insecurity, and other human frailties than any other hall of learning he had worked in. He had not expected the use of markers over words to provoke such outrage. This talented but, I imagine, somewhat introverted man believed that his dictionary would be debated on its merits, rather than as part of a discussion about Timor's linkages with Portugal and its place in the world. In the end, following a dispute over unpaid fees, he took early retirement. I tried to cheer him up by telling him how useful I and no doubt many others had found his work when learning Tetun, but it was small comfort to him. 'If I had my way over again, I wish I had never met the Timorese,' he said. He sounded like a melancholy Portuguese administrator.

What happened to Geoffrey Hull could be read as a salutary parable about the perils of foreigners trying to do too much, too fast. Like CAVR, the National Institute was a place with Timorese titularly in charge, but where many foreigners did a lot of the work, at a pace and intensity that generated mountains of paper but not much understanding.

Chapter Seven
Learning the Language

When I first went to Dili, I felt very awkward because of my inability to communicate with Timorese beyond nods, sheepish grins, and pointing at items on a menu or in a fridge. I had been hired to research a paper on veterans, but felt like a disingenuous charlatan to be pronouncing on a subject when I couldn't even exchange basic pleasantries with my interviewees. I knew the Dalai Lama had said you could get a good conversation going just by staying silent and smiling, but his strategy wasn't working for me. I was convinced that I would need to learn to speak some Tetun if I was going to enjoy my spell in the country in any way — never mind contribute anything useful to it.

I could take the embarrassment no more, so I went to Tetun school, which was located at Timor Aid, the offices of which were just beside the old Hotel Turismo and the new walled compound for the prime minister. The building was previously the home of Maria do Ceu Lopes Federer, the daughter of a Timorese woman and a Portuguese firebrand who had been exiled to the island of Atauro, and was now the headquarters of the Timor Aid NGO that Maria had started. My teacher was a small bearded man called Alfredo Gama, who showed up to the first lesson wearing a T-shirt with the FRETILIN logo. Although the party had governed the country from independence to 2007, it had just been ousted in favour of a coalition of parties led by CNRT (the National Council of Timorese Resistance) the political party of Xanana Gusmao. Naturally, I assumed he was a FRETILIN supporter. But the next day, he showed up in a T-shirt bearing the colours of CNRT, their fierce political rivals. On the third day, he was resplendent wearing the logo of yet another party. It was all very confusing, so I asked him who he supported. 'If you go to all the rallies, you get free food and clothes,' he said. This was my very first indication of the fluidity of party affiliations in Timor-Leste.

Alfredo was a really enthusiastic teacher, but I must have been a really tiresome student. My head hurt trying to remember all the new words and how to pronounce them; it made me wonder how I'd ever managed to learn all the words that I knew in English. It was difficult to recall the words for items in the classroom such as 'desk', 'chair', and 'window', to say nothing of how one said 'on the desk' or 'under the chair'. But I was determined to succeed, and studied and studied as if my life depended upon it.

I spent a few hours with Alfredo each morning, and had little baby conversations with him — no doubt maiming one word for each one I pronounced correctly. I spent the afternoons with the newspapers and Geoffrey Hull's dictionary, looking up nearly every word and writing the English version in the line above the article, trying to piece together elements of a story in a way that would make sense to my English-language-wired brain. Over time, I came to glean that this was, in fact, the point: English is not easily compatible with Tetun; this incongruence is indicative not only of the different national mindsets, but also of their different frames of reference and senses of what is important. There is no differentiation between 'he' and 'she' in Tetun, although there are two different ways of saying 'we' and 'you' — which, I later discovered, was common within the huge family of Austronesian languages that Tetun belongs to. There are three different ways of addressing an individual, each one indicating the speaker's position in relation to the person being addressed. There are no verb tenses, but a much more complicated way of coding family relationships than exists in, say, English. You can't, for example, say 'brother' and 'sister' without including the age relationship. There are at least six different ways, as far as I know, to express the word 'cousin', reflecting Timorese kinship categories. From the perspective of an English speaker, the language appears on many occasions to lend itself to ambiguity, inference, veiled speech, metaphor, and analogy. The late anthropologist Tom Terik used the term *lia sasaluk* (wrapped-up language) to describe the way that Tetun speakers on the south coast disguise meanings in their speech.

At last, after a few months of writing and re-writing words on flash cards, I found that I could get the gist of a newspaper article without consulting a dictionary, and could follow in basic terms what was being said on the TV news. My little baby-language steps didn't become bounding conversational strides that traversed our cultural gaps, but I was well pleased that I was able to communicate relatively clearly. I remember one of my first 'substantive' conversations at a photocopy shop where I found I had enough vocabulary to talk about the Timorese living in Northern Ireland. 'Do the Timorese speak English there?' I asked the man behind the counter, whose brother was working over there. 'They must do, or otherwise their life would be very difficult,' he said, and I resolved to find out whether they did. I remember walking out of the shop practically punching the air with joy at having strung sufficient words together in a coherent-enough way so that someone could understand me.

After a while, no waitress, taxi driver, or passer-by in the street was safe from my semi-stilted conversational repartee. Almost everyone I met was extremely understanding and forgiving — much more tolerant than I imagined I would have been, had the situation been reversed. I learned more and more each day. The headquarters of one of the parties in the new governing coalition was close by, and I whiled away hours drinking black, sugary coffee in good china cups with a bunch of very patient, gap-toothed elderly men who told me their stories about how the old politics and relationships underlie today's politics.

It was there that I got my first sense of just how bombastic Timorese political rhetoric sounded to the un-tuned ear of an English speaker. Party supporters were called *militantes* (militants), and their platform alternated between the messianic and the incredibly vague. I asked the old codgers what the party's intentions were, now that they were in office: 'It is clear: our policy is to save the nation', they told me with the utmost sincerity.

I came to appreciate how body parts and topographical features had both their literal meanings and other meanings. Some are extensions of meaning akin to those found in other languages. *Fulan* (moon) also means 'month', and *ulun* (head) also means those 'at the head', or 'rulers'. I believe similar constructions are to be found in many Indo–European languages. When you add an adjective, the meaning can change quite drastically, which thoroughly confused me at the start — probably because I was translating too literally. One of my companions told me he had *anin aat*, and I was delighted to realise that I knew what this meant, but less delighted by its literal translation: 'bad wind'. I marvelled at why he would be so open about his flatulence, until I looked up the phrase in the dictionary later and discovered that it meant he had an 'allergy'. He was very pleased when I gave him some 'sacred bark to drink' — the literal translation of what we would call anti-histamine tablets —

to help stave off his sneezing.

Each day, the papers would be full of tongue-tying and obtuse bluster, making Alfredo Reinado's mountain-top statements seem like models of clarity and conciseness by comparison. Politicians were always promising that something would happen, which very rarely did according to their promised schedule. Members of parliament would call for national unity and social harmony. Military and police commanders would 'guarantee' security, even though the actions of their troops and officers were oftentimes the chief cause of *in*security. The language was, all things considered, relatively easy and fun to learn, but it was sometimes extremely difficult to penetrate it enough to find out what was behind it. I came to think that this ambiguity quite suited the Timorese political discourse: if everyone spoke in generalities, no one could really be held to account for very much.

The irony, of course, is that many of those who had come to Timor-Leste with much grander goals than I had — nothing short of helping to build the institutions of a modern state — found relatively modest undertakings, such as reading the newspaper or engaging in general 'passing the time of day' conversations, to be completely beyond them. A self-proclaimed policing expert of five years' tenure who appeared to take her make-up tips from Elvira, Mistress of the Dark, hectored me on how little I knew about Timorese culture and how much she knew in comparison. As it turned out, she was unable to ask for a cigarette lighter. When I asked for one on her behalf, which required knowing the sum total of three Tetun words, she glowered at me, her expression a curious mix of jealousy and insecurity. I once watched a senior mover and shaker who worked in a large 'capacity-building' program for Timorese government institutions berating a young luggage-handler at the airport, and becoming ever more irked because the Timorese couldn't comprehend his nasal Australian English. Perhaps he wasn't shouting loudly enough. I remember thinking, *Good luck trying to explain the concept of a budget if you can't explain how to shift some bags.*

The only word that many *malae* seem able to say confidently is *mana*, the Timorese word for 'big sister', which they use to summon waiting staff at restaurants. As it turns out, unless the person serving the food happens to be older than them, this is the wrong word. Tetun has different words for family members, such as older or younger sisters, depending upon the age relationships.

Some *malae* do speak very good Tetun — much, much more proficiently than I ever managed to achieve. But, in the main, donors and international organisations (and many of the people who work in them) assign little importance to language, and regard it as a pesky nuisance, rather than considering it an essential building block in making themselves useful and relevant in Timor-Leste. I used to marvel at how some *malae* would find excuse after excuse for not attending Tetun-language classes; there seemed always an 'important meeting' in the expat coffee shop scheduled at the exact time they were meant to go to their lesson. Some ambassadors, people with much fuller schedules, seemed able to find the time, so why couldn't they? Some grew haughty at the suggestion that they should attend classes, and drew on an example of somewhere they'd worked previously without having to deal with such inconveniences, as justification. Their disdain and lack of respect for learning was a thin veil for their insecurity and self-consciousness. The attempts of international capacity-builders and their Timorese counterparts to interact with each other reminded me of awkward wallflower moments I had had at teenage discos.

The fact that English is the mother tongue of the capacity-builders and that Tetun is the language of those whose capacity is meant to be 'built' presents basic challenges of being able to define the vague and indeterminate goal of 'capacity', in the first place. This linguistic gap results in a highly subjective approach to diplomacy, capacity-building, and technical assistance, based on the foreigner's preference for interacting with Timorese who can speak English. All too often, it is the few English-speaking Timorese officials who are sought out as counterparts — who, given their language skills, often tend to be pulled in many directions, and are not likely to have the time or need to have their capacity 'built'. Non-English-speaking Timorese get nods and smiles instead.

Documents in English are not translated as a matter of course, but are sent out in the (frequently vain) hope that someone who speaks English will pick them up. Few relationships can develop without the ability to interact, and discuss and stew over new ideas, but this relatively obvious fact is ignored frequently. No one would expect a Timorese police officer or public servant who spoke no English to be successful in effecting change in Canberra, Dublin, or other capitals, and yet this idea seems perfectly acceptable in reverse. In my experience, those who didn't speak any Tetun seemed to be the most zealous in peddling the caricature that it is somehow not a 'proper' language. A puffed-up figure in the International Stabilisation Force based in Timor told me that Tetun was an 'agricultural' language — whatever that meant — and didn't have enough words and concepts to be used as a language of governance and the law. He was speaking very confidently and knowledgably until, about ten minutes into the conversation, I realised that he didn't speak a word of Tetun.

The need to improve Tetun-language skills among long-term staff is now a boilerplate recommendation that emerges from any review or evaluation conducted about the country, but organisations have been ducking effective implementation of this suggestion for years. My pet theory is that this is because the heads of the organisations in Timor-Leste fear that they might have to learn it themselves. In 2010, the United Nations undertook to provide introductory Tetun to its incoming UNPOL. It was a belated recognition of the importance of being able to converse with the people they were working with, but it was a barely kept promise. Over a year later, just fifty UNPOL out of fifteen hundred had been trained, for a grand total of two hours each. Even a master linguist such as Geoffrey Hull would struggle to attain basic linguistic proficiency in such a short course.

Following Alfredo, my second Tetun teacher was not only an expert guide to the Tetun language, but also to the culture that the language gives access to. His name was Anacleto da Costa Ribeiro, and I got to know him when I worked in the office of Francisco Guterres.

My wife said that Anacleto would be a good poker player; he gave nothing away for about the first one hundred occasions you met him. I think I was a few weeks into sharing an office with him before he uttered his first words to me. He probably had me pegged as just another *malae* who would stay for a few months and then leave, frustrated at somehow not being able to turn around the functioning of the entire ministry. Perhaps because I stayed a bit longer than most, we got to know each other a little better, and he delighted in impressing me by peppering his conversations with the slightly out-of-date English idiomatic expressions he had learned when studying in New Zealand over a decade earlier. 'Keep the ball rolling' and 'piece of cake' were a couple of his favourites, which he'd say as he peered over the stacks of paper weighing down his desk — none of which had been filed since he moved into the office. We became good friends, and later it was he who suggested our son's second name, Murak.

Anacleto had been educated in three languages. As a child, he was taught in a Portuguese school and, when he was in his early twenties, he studied linguistics in Indonesian at university in Bali with, among others, Fernando 'La Sama'. Anacleto was the dorm-room captain who had to cover for his friends when they sneaked off in the middle of the night for secret political meetings with other activists. Along the way, he mastered English for his master's course in development studies in New Zealand.

His day job as adviser to the secretary of state involved feigning interest in sectoral committees, joining working groups, and attending countless meetings with the eager foreigners that are regularly visited upon English-speaking Timorese. His real passion, though, was developing Tetun as a proud language in its own right, and ridding Timorese of what he believed was a post-colonial sense that it was somehow a second-class language. He thought Tetun should be used instead of Portuguese as a matter of establishing national identity and as a means of expressing cultural separateness. By now, I had no doubt that Tetun is an indelible link with the past. The language transfers values from the past to current generations; it conveys what is important and, conversely, what is not. The Timorese work within a language that has some concepts that we don't have in English. Conversely, Tetun lacks some that we do have. There is no authentically Tetun word for 'corruption', even if concepts of poor governance and official wrongdoing exist (for which they use *korrupsaun*), but there are countless specific words to describe different elements of a traditional ceremony. 'Warm the tent', for instance, means have a little party before the big one.

Anacleto taught me many words and phrases; but, perhaps more importantly, he taught me to see the language, not just as a form of words to communicate with, but as a looking glass reflecting societal mores and what the Timorese deem important. 'It's never good to say *hau* (I),' too often, he said, as this marks one out as too individualistic. 'Best to say *ita* (the collective 'we').'

Occasionally, I would let slip to him how frustrated I was by what I naïvely thought were terribly important policy processes being either postponed or run aground entirely. At such times, he always had an idiom to soothe me. Things that I found deeply troublesome and that led me to erupt in a po-faced paroxysm — such as why-oh-why did Timorese drive state cars on the weekend, when they were not allowed to — would be played down with a patient smile. 'Family is much more important here,' he would explain. 'If I had a car and didn't share it with them or allow them to travel in it, they would think badly of me. They would think that I was *halo a'an*' — something that would probably translate into English as "far too big for my boots".' He could probably also have mentioned that the Timorese have seen United Nations staff and others gadding around in their cars on Saturdays and Sundays; so, as we might say, 'What's good for the goose …'

He would sometimes chide me about watching the clock too much — which was ironic, given that, by Western standards, I am not a particularly punctual person. 'Internationals are always interested in punctuality and things running on time but, for us, that's not as important,' he said. The longer I stayed, the more I could see his point. In a place where family is paramount, of course it's more important to attend a family funeral than to linger around the office to attend a meeting with a visiting delegation from some country or international organisation, and answer questions that have been answered many times before. 'Time is elastic here,' he'd explain.

Anacleto's spoken English was really excellent, but he did ask my advice on editing the English in a bilingual dictionary of idioms that he had prepared. Idioms have a way of drawing the listener's attention to certain things while pushing others into the background, and the dictionary was useful to me as another window into our socio-cultural differences and similarities. I was happy to help, and also happy that no large-scale editing was required. Unusually for a person for whom English was not his first language, Anacleto's written English was on a par with his spoken abilities. Some idioms were identical, such as 'to play a dirty game' (*halo jogada foer*) and 'to wash one's hands of' (*fase liman*). The latter was derived from the Easter story, and is — in both languages — a euphemism for disclaiming personal responsibility.

At the same time, another washing-based idiom had a meaning that made no literal sense out of context. To 'wash plates' (*fase bikan*) meant, idiomatically, to have a small party after the large party in order to thank the family members who had done the washing up. Some were amazingly specific: 'dog smells bones' referred to the feeling of pleasure when someone showed up at (we might say, 'gate-crashed') a party un-announced. Other idioms referred to activities that needed to happen *before* a party, or to the various names for different ceremonies, such as *kore metan*, where one changed out of the black garb that had been worn for a year after a family member's death. This was an occasion marked by an almighty dancing-till-dawn hoedown that would require enthusiastic tent-warming beforehand and concerted plate-washing afterwards. Perhaps my favourite of the lot — one that always seemed to delight Timorese when I said it, as it was drawn from cultural practices that they were convinced *malae* knew nothing about — was *han isin, sikat ruin*: eat the flesh, keep the bones, which is customarily said to the host when exiting the party. It sort of means that the score is settled and that everyone is in the clear with each other. Eventually, this replaced *asu hosu* ('farting dog') — meaning to start something and not finish it because one does not have the dedication required

— as my favourite of all the Timorese idioms.

Anacleto was adamant that language shaped thought, which was something I'd never considered until he said it, and something that I then thought was a fairly uncontroversial assertion until I realised that academics have been ding-donging over this issue for decades. The question as to whether any language affects or determines the way that the speaker thinks is the subject of rancorous, and oftentimes inaccessible, debate among linguists. After spending the better part of a whole day surfing through the waves of their virulent debates on some language list-serves, I had nearly lost whatever abilities I had had to think in English.

The dominant position in the language debate is that language does not shape thought, and that all languages share equal traits. This view is most commonly associated with the polymath and long-time Timor solidarity activist Professor Noam Chomsky, probably the most renowned linguist alive today. Chomsky argues that all humans — no matter whether born in Belfast or Baucau — have an innate, universal grammar which, in effect, means that the differences between languages are relatively superficial. An opposing view, in its most extreme form, suggests that language reflects cultural conventions and habits. This is arguing that, in effect, a native English speaker from Northern Ireland would, even if he or she learned Makassae fluently, struggle to fit in should he or she somehow end up living in a thatched hut off the beaten track in the Timorese mountains. This is a proposition that emphasises cultural difference, but one potential downside is that it could be read as reinforcing the barmy generalisations about Tetun as somehow not being a fit and proper language — an assertion from which Anacleto and other Tetun speakers would rightly recoil.

The linguist Guy Deutscher, author of *Through the Language Glass*, engages in no such essentialism. Indeed, research on the impact of culture and environment on language is still so relatively rudimentary that only saloon-room philosophers could reach definitive conclusions on such a topic. Deutscher's conclusions are modest and well summarised: 'The concepts we treat as distinct, the information our mother tongue continually forces us to specify, the details it requires us to be attentive to, and the repeated associations it imposes upon us — all of these habits of speech can create habits of mind that affect more than merely the knowledge of language itself.' We are all, to some extent, what we speak, which is an entirely different proposition from believing that one language is somehow superior to another.

So now it is a matter of filling in the blanks in Tetun and standardising the language, rather than somehow dismissing it out of hand as not fit-for-purpose. This is easier said than done, given that no one seems to be directing language development from the top, or affording it real importance. The Indonesian language was in a somewhat similar un-homogenised state when Indonesia became independent. Many, but not all, people within the vast territory of the new state spoke it fluently, but there were no rules governing standard usage, spelling, or orthography. The state of Israel also invested deeply in reviving Hebrew so that it became a national language. One doesn't detect the same degree of zeal among sufficient numbers of people in Dili. Perhaps the biggest risk in trying to cater for all constituencies and simultaneously communicate with all parts of the globe is that no one will understand them. The bishop of Dili says that Timorese speak 'Tetunbahasagues', a mixture of many languages, none of which are spoken well, and most of which are unintelligible beyond the island itself — except perhaps to the Timorese diaspora.

The problem is not just language: it's also education. Many civil servants have difficulty expressing themselves in written Tetun, or in any other of the official languages. I once saw five civil servants work for hours on a document on their computer screen after a delegation from Angola had breezed through Dili on a 'fact-finding' mission earlier that day and had dangled the prospects of some free trips to Luanda to study community-conflict prevention. Preparing the letter took the quintet all afternoon. I was curious to see the end product, which I thought would be a few pages of text at the very least. It turned out to be two lines saying, 'We would like to go to Angola to study', topped and tailed by honorifics and titles. Words were misspelled, and even I could see that the grammar was rickety.

Although there are some Timorese like Anacleto who write persuasively in Tetun, they are very much in the minority. Despite all the oil money gushing around, there seems to be little attention at the top devoted to the issues of how to train civil servants to work in Tetun, or to ensure that teachers impart a standard form of the language to their students. As we shall see in the next chapter, much of the state's money is going elsewhere, with a concentration, arguably, on short-term fixes rather than long-term solutions.

Chapter Eight
The Lure of Easy Money

In 2011, the finance minister of Timor-Leste, Emilia Pires, gave a short interview to *Monocle*, the travel magazine of choice for those with high levels of frequent-flyer points and enough disposable income to splash out on high-end Swiss watches. 'If the first decade of the 21st century belonged to China,' she declared, 'then the second decade will belong to Timor-Leste.' It was an extraordinary statement from a minister in a country ranked 120th out of 169 in the United Nations Human Development Index, with a population of barely one million people. But is reflective of the reach-for-the-stars philosophy of the current crop of Timorese leaders.

Such nationalistic bluster is fuelled by the oil and gas reserves in the Timor Sea. Timor-Leste is the beneficiary of the resource lottery: over three-quarters of its GDP comes from oil and gas reserves located in the sea between its southern coast and Australia. In English, this stretch of water is known as the Timor Sea, and it is known to sailors for its rough and treacherous swirls. In Tetun, the water is known as *tasi mane* (the male sea), a place where stories handed down through the generations have told of both a great source of wealth and *lulik*, a Tetun word meaning 'sacredness'. Many women still do not swim in the sea, for their ancestors warned that if they went in with their thighs exposed, they would be drawn into the sea by a male wave and taken away, never to be seen again.

The billions of dollars that sit in the sea have the potential to transform Timor-Leste from Asia's poorest country to a much more affluent one. Flush with revenue, the government is trying to spend the nation out of poverty. In the 2003–04 financial year, the budget was US$74 million; less than ten years later, it was US$1.8 billion — a nearly thirty-two-fold increase. Almost all of it derives from exporting the country's non-renewable oil and gas reserves. In aspiration and direction, Timor-Leste's leaders seem to perceive Dili as more like the capital of a fellow petro-state, such as Doha in Qatar, than an aid-dependent 'post-conflict' country, such as Kathmandu in Nepal. Nowadays, the money in the national government's bank account far outstrips the amount given to it in foreign aid.

Dili is in the giddy grip of a liquid-gold rush. The minister's statement is indicative not just of a government looking to cement its own prestige, but also of a people whose development dreams don't always seem grounded in the reality around them. Money sloshes around the capital like wine in a decanter, and signs of capitalist consumerism are there for all to see. Hotels and eating-places are filled with newly ennobled Timorese businessmen who are fast getting rich by receiving (though not necessarily always executing) government contracts. The gas-fuelled *nouveau riche* is now the majority in many restaurants previously frequented only by *malae*. The pricey Nautilus restaurant on Dili's beachfront, for example, used to be the place where only international advisers would go for a leisurely bottle of wine, imported steak, and long whinges about how difficult life was in the tropics. Many well-heeled Timorese businessmen may now be found lunching there, sipping wine both ostentatiously and self-consciously while their over-priced bottle chills next to them in the cooler stand. There seems to be little intrinsic value attached to money, although clearly it conveys much status. I remember complimenting a Timorese businessman on his sassy new eyeglasses. They were a bargain: 'only US$750!' he exclaimed. A new shopping plaza enables the Timorese elite to spend even more money on luxury goods without having to take the flight to Bali. Wedding parties are ever more elaborate and ever more costly. Models strutted the catwalk at a national fashion show in 2012.

Recipients of government contracts are lavishly renovating their houses into garish mansions, Indonesian-elite style. Some of the wealthiest have second homes in Bali. People exit banks with plates so laden with dollars that they sometimes need help from an extra person to carry out all the loot. The capital's streets are choked with traffic, and one can see quite a few pimped-up new cars such as Hummers with tinted windows and fancy rims that would not look out of place dropping off movie stars at an awards ceremony. The drivers of the gleaming cars in ministerial convoys turn on their sirens to part the traffic jams so that the occupants inside can get to their next meeting on time. Thousands of new motorbikes scoot around the potholes in the roads. Dili's population is increasing, as more and more young Timorese from rural districts flock there. There are few paid jobs out in the districts, and rural Timorese arrive looking for a slice of the action. However, they often find that the reality does not live up to their dreams. Many of the newcomers find themselves getting frustrated and jealous, living with family members in already overcrowded houses.

The money has bought peace, at least for a while. At first blush, Dili is a safer, happier, more content place than the fearful city I moved to in 2007. When I first arrived, it was hard to get one of the yellow-coloured taxis to take you anywhere if it was later than six o'clock in the evening; the drivers did not feel safe being out of their homes after dark. Now, the cabs operate at all hours. The major problem facing the city today is not crazed rebels, but crazy driving.

The waterfront in Dili is thronging with families and young couples spending money on the little stalls that sell chicken satays, grilled fish, and beer. Dili now has a baby-clothing store, a dry cleaner, an aquarium shop, a driving range, and a cellar door — sure mercantile signs of disposable income. By the time I left, it even had two Turkish kebab shops. Dili has a better atmosphere, and the people look happier. It is easy to harrumph and shake one's head about all the improvident spending, but the evidence of current contentment is there for all to see, albeit for only a fraction of the population to enjoy.

The question, however, is whether today's smiles and good times are a temporary bubble inflated by oil and gas revenues, or the start of something more permanent. Does Timor-Leste risk sliding into the problems faced by other countries that have struck it rich through the sheer luck of owning oil and gas resources, only to find themselves beset later on by a range of unwelcome and unexpected problems? The adverse effects include high inflation, poor planning, inequality between the haves and the have-nots, a slide into indebtedness, neglect of human resources, and failure to build up more sustainable and labour-intensive parts of the economy. The challenge, ultimately, is to minimise corruption and cronyism, and the wasteful funding of prestige projects, and instead to invest in the human capital needed to run an effective government, and to develop an inclusive, equitable, sustainable economy. The presence of oil and gas deposits also frequently poisons relations with neighbouring countries over boundary lines. And academic researchers who have studied the data have found that wars are statistically more likely to occur in resource-rich states.

Economists call this blight the 'resource curse', and there are many sombre examples of it occurring in small and fledgling states whose mix of young institutions and resource abundance closely resembles Timor-Leste's. In places such as Nigeria, Gabon, and Nauru, the result is often a steep decline in living standards over the long term. There has even been a marked drop in per-capita GDP over the last thirty years in Saudi Arabia, the country generally considered to have the world's largest reserves of oil. Will Timor-Leste squander its oil and gas wealth, instead of stewarding it wisely for future generations? Or will it become like Norway, generally cited as the only country to have avoided falling into the resource trap?

Dili certainly has the feel of a cautionary case study in a development-economics textbook. To be sure, certain features of Timor-Leste reduce some of the factors that can give rise to the resource curse. The country's decision to adopt the United States dollar as its currency means that the developing nation will not suffer from exchange-rate problems caused by the influx of oil money. The decision of the first government, following restoration of independence, to establish a sovereign wealth fund — in which money is tucked away — is considered international best practice.

But other current policies seem classic exemplars of what governments in these situations should not do. The government allocates more money to scholarships for Timorese students overseas than it does for operating the national university. Newly created companies, some of the directors of which are related to some members of the governing coalition, import hundreds of millions of dollars' worth of rice. In contrast, much, much less money is allocated to boosting local agriculture and food production. Some US$100 million worth of prefabricated houses bought from Indonesia have been erected, instead of building new homes with Timorese wood and stone. Large amounts of money are allocated for cultural ceremonies: US$5 million was allocated in the 2012 budget to commemorate the centenary of Boaventura's revolt. The 2011 inflation figure was over 15 per cent. The country has a very high trade deficit and, beyond coffee and mung beans (a type of legume often found in vegan restaurants, and very common in south-east Asian cuisines), it has little to export other than oil and gas, which is a finite resource, while the vast majority of the goods in the country are imported. Imports are 24 times the value of exports ... and virtually all paid for with oil money.

Tourism is a potentially lucrative source of revenue for the Timorese; I remember a grizzled old Aussie telling me that present-day Timor had a natural beauty that reminded him of Bali before the mass influx of foreigners. This prospect has yet to be developed. Beyond a few hardy backpackers, some divers, and a couple of tour companies that run scenic excursions via car and motorbike, the industry is virtually non-existent at present.

Some of the expanded budget is, however, going to where it is needed most. The US$30 individual payments that old men and women receive each month helps make life just that bit more bearable. But a lot of money has gone on less essential items. Flashy equipment is procured when cheaper alternatives would probably have done just as well. Timorese military personnel and police officers drive around in top-of-the-range pick-ups which, with windows down and stereo blaring, zoom around the streets to little obvious purpose beyond stoking the driver's ego.

Other purchases were sanctioned with even less thought as to their utility. Each police station in the country was given a computer and printer in 2009 that, in the absence of electricity, quickly became little more than dusty ornaments. The Ministry of Agriculture bought truck-loads of tractors that they gave to politically connected farmers, but the farmers didn't know how to use or repair them, and many of the tractors fell over on the steep, mountainous terrain. Most of these purchases now rust by the side of the road, apparently because the recipients refused to put fuel in the tank, which they thought it was the government's job to provide. In 2009 and 2010, Timor-Leste failed to meet the 'anti-corruption' scores needed to access the United States' Millennium Challenge Account, and then gave up trying, as so much money was rolling in from the oil and gas fields. In 2012, the army said it needed helicopters.

Buying physical things such as cars, trucks, and planes is relatively easy, but it is more difficult to use money to develop intangibles such as managerial abilities and technocratic competence in the civil service, especially when these skills are not necessarily prioritised or deemed important. Training courses are sometimes postponed or not attended with much interest — a sure sign of the lack of importance placed on professional development by employees at all levels. Money buys short-cut fixes, and solves short-term political problems, but educational attainment is not something that can be easily bought. The government hires national and international 'advisers', whose role in reality is less to 'advise' Timorese civil servants on how to do their job and more to do the job for them. Many are earning twenty, forty, and sixty times the salary of state officials, whose own salaries have risen dramatically in the last few years. By contrast, 3.2 per cent of the 2012 state budget was allocated to health — an abominably low figure.

Over the four years I spent there, I became more convinced that the Timorese government thinks of foreigners as a well-paid worker class rather than as 'capacity-builders'. One of my main jobs when I worked in a Timorese government office was to write letters in English to the United Nations mission, and today there are many others doing the same. For example, the government's press releases are sent out in perfect English in the name of a fifty-something minister, Agio Pereira, who was a long-time activist for Timorese independence and a noted crooner. He once released a cassette tape of protest songs entitled 'I'm Still Fighting'. His press releases are apparently written by a public-relations firm based in the east coast of Australia, which allegedly commands a handsome annual fee for dashing them off.

Sometimes you get the impression that the billions of dollars in the wealth fund are burning a hole in the government's pocket. Former president Ramos-Horta once offered to use the money to buy Portuguese bonds, describing it as a shrewd investment shortly before the former colonial power's credit status was downgraded to 'junk'. Timor-Leste is even subsidising Portugal in order to borrow some of its police officers for training programs — something for which the former colonisers previously paid. The Portuguese judges and language teachers in the country are being paid for by Dili, not Lisbon. The Timorese government has donated funds to other countries, including contributions to the clean-up following the 2008 earthquakes in China, the 2011 floods in Australia, and the tsunami in Japan in the same year. The government even offered to send a crack team of police and military to Japan to help out — an offer that the administration in Tokyo declined with thanks.

Other money is spent asserting Timor-Leste's place in the world. Timor-Leste is chair and driving member of the G7+, a lobby group of 'fragile states' that assertively tells donor governments how little they know about the countries in which they are working. It is a good idea. As a recipient country, Timor-Leste has first-hand experience of donor money not being used effectively. But, at the same time, the group's rhetorical aspirations of giving voice to the voiceless can sometimes be hard to square with the fact that meetings take place in the sort of expensive international hotels and conference venues that the aid industry relishes meeting in. They are thereby supporting the very behaviour that they are trying to change.

Everyone knows that discussions about poverty cost a lot of money. The Aid Effectiveness Directorate is the brainchild of the minister of finance, Emilia Pires. Its job is to monitor how development funding is spent in Timor-Leste. As it happens, at least some of the staff in the directorate that expounds the importance of 'local ownership' are foreigners, paid for by donor organisations.

The goal of the government's glossy *Strategic Development Plan 2011–30* is nothing less than to transform what is still Asia's poorest nation into an upper-to-middle-income country in less than twenty years. The extremely ambitious plans will require even higher allocations of public spending, and will necessitate borrowing money from other states — something that a previous government resolutely did not do. The fuzzy blueprint has something of the air of modernisation plans from half a century ago; it is as if the Timorese government believes that ideals dreamt up in air-conditioned offices (much of the document was produced in Jakarta) can create a nirvana symbolised by the young children who smile out from many pages of the publication. Arguably, there's not much of a plan in the document at all — just lists of visions, targets, and goals. How to get from here to there is barely mentioned. You have to take a lot on faith.

The goal is laudable, and nothing less than the resilient and hard-pressed Timorese deserve. There are hopes for everything, from the teaching of architecture in seven new universities throughout the country, to high-speed Internet throughout a land that currently has intermittent or no electricity. Also envisaged are a food supply that exceeds demand, a universal social-security system, an extensive network of land and marine national parks, a national ring-road, and laws regulating almost every conceivable practice and behaviour. But is it really laudable to invite failure through setting unrealistic goals? The government is moving so fast that it has not even had time to translate the promise of what is to be achieved from English and Portuguese into Tetun, thereby ensuring that the plan is a mystery to most of the government officials who are theoretically intended to implement it. Hours before he praised it in public, I heard a donor complain that the Timorese were living in 'la-la land' with this plan.

Another side effect of the resource dependency is that it is turning the social contract on its head, and raising expectations to artificially high levels. Most states can only finance their operations and services by collecting taxes from their people. In Timor-Leste, which currently combines one of the lowest tax bases and collection rates in the world with the highest rate of dependency on resource revenues, it doesn't work that way. There is an expectation that citizens who don't need to put anything in are entitled to get a lot out. The result is a dangerous dependency, and what scholars have called a 'rentier' economy, in which the state generates its revenues, not from taxing its citizens, but from selling off its own resource base. In 2011, civil servants were given an extra month's pay across the board, irrespective of whether each individual deserved it or not. Some surely did, but not all. A year later, it was announced that, upon retirement, civil servants would receive final-salary pensions — a decision that was further unlikely to inculcate a performance-based culture in government ministries.

In Timor-Leste, barrel-loads of money are often raided to resolve problems. The problems from the 2006 crisis included internally destroyed homes, and displaced people and petitioners who were bought off through the doling out of money rather than having the root causes of their situations addressed and resolved. Subsequent problems are solved with an even higher subsidy, which, in turn, creates more demand. The renegade soldier Gastao Salsinha called a press conference to say he felt hard done by because he and others who had been jailed for the attacks on the president and prime minister never received the US$8,500 payment given to other petitioners. He'd seen contracts handed out to others, including a multi-million dollar electricity contract to a former comrade-in-arms. He was angry in a way that we all are when someone comes into money and we don't. 'In many countries, you would feel really lucky just to be pardoned,' I reminded him one day. He said simply that he saw so many others benefiting who had done much worse than he had. On balance, I can see his point. As I was finishing the initial draft of this chapter, I read that the money allocated to pensions for veterans in the 2012 budget was higher than that allocated to the entire ministry of education.

This blank-cheque approach to problem-solving not only distorts the state's relationships with its citizens, but it also almost completely inhibits private business initiatives. There is little incentive for entrepreneurial inventiveness; instead, every effort is focused on having the right connections with someone in the government, in order to secure a juicy government contract. At the same time, there's very little productive business — hence the import dependency and high unemployment — because getting a state contract is so much easier than processing or manufacturing something, and having to deal with customers and competition. Who you know is clearly as much, or perhaps more, of a determinant of whether you will be awarded a contract than are your demonstrated levels of technical or professional expertise. Some of the veterans of the liberation war became wealthy businessmen overnight.

When I worked there, the *de facto* residence of most of the arrivistes was the cavernous Hotel Timor coffee lobby, where they whiled away most days swapping stories over espressos, with the yellowed ashtrays on the tables getting ever fuller. The air was preternaturally thick with the smell of clove-infused tobacco, so that I often wondered how the paintings on the walls managed to escape nicotine stains. Once, I got chatting with my Facebook friend, the former soldier turned hit-squad leader turned business impresario, Rai Los. I asked him how much building experience he had had before he set up his own construction company that had become the recipient of substantial government contracts. He gave a sort of shrug-smile, and we went on to talk about something else. Rai Los is a major donor to the party that won most seats in the last election. Timor-Leste is ranked 168 out of 183 countries in the World Bank's 2012 *Doing Business* report.

The pernicious and perverse effects of this resource-revenue dependence are understood by a diverse group that includes learned economists in far-off universities and residents of the Niger Delta, but they are downplayed by members of the government. Like most people on the up, they're not in the mood for lectures on fiscal responsibility. They know what they're doing, they say; the foreign naysayers don't know what they're talking about. Yes, Timor-Leste is using its resources, but what is the alternative: keep the oil and gas in the ground, and rack up lots of debts to world financial institutions and other countries? Yes, Timor-Leste knows that doom-mongers say there will be no money for future generations, but how do you even get to the future if you don't invest in today? It's true, there is a heavy emphasis on infrastructure, but how do you develop other capabilities without good transport connections? The refutations of the resource-curse thesis are delivered passionately, and questions about corruption are dismissed with the wave of a hand.

One day, curious to see how far the government largesse extended, I went down to the southern coast of the Viqueque district — one of the places closest to the resource reserves. Leaving the crowded streets of Dili, I quickly discovered that this boom is unequally concentrated in the capital. To bump along the roads to the districts is to turn back the clock. To be sure, there is the odd new (Chinese-run) minimarket here and there, and there are lots of motorbikes, but the great majority of Timorese beyond the capital remain subsistence farmers. Many continue to live in deep, grinding poverty. It can sometimes feel as though there are two completely different countries within the one national territory. Dotting the hillsides are grey pylon poles without wires; this is the first step in a project to bring electricity to the countryside that is years late in delivering on its commitment. The project is a parable about how easily acquired money can quickly be wasted. A Chinese company 'won' the secret tender to build the power plants that would generate the electricity. The technology that the Timorese government opted for was based on second-hand 'heavy oil' generators — an outmoded, potentially catastrophic technology environmentally. The government went ahead with the contract, unswayed by the knowledge that unwanted by-products of heavy oil include high levels of pollution, soil erosion, and acid rain. The project was years past schedule and three times over budget. The ever-more-portly and ever-less-convincing secretary of state for electricity appeared on the TV on regular occasions, 'guaranteeing' that switch-on would happen soon. His blandishments were believed by fewer and fewer viewers. Auditors discovered the plant was in a state of neglect, with shoddy workmanship, gross inattention to detail, and cost overruns at every turn. Rubbish was being strewn on the beaches. No wonder that the opposition made a pun of the government's acronym, AMP. The government, they said, did not stand for Alliance for Majority in Parliament, but *Ahi Mate Permanente* (the electricity is always off).

In the southern towns where the government promises to transform the economy by building a 'petroleum corridor' consisting of a supply base for offshore oil operations, a liquefied-natural-gas plant, a 150-kilometre highway, and an oil refinery, there are high expectations. To date, though, few obvious benefits seemed to have trickled down to the population. The promises of thousands of jobs seem grossly over-estimated, as not much labour is needed to process and support offshore gas extraction. Because of the highly specialised nature of the industry, few Timorese will have the qualifications in chemical engineering necessary to be able to work there. And even if these plants are built, they will generate only a few non-skilled jobs, such as security guards, maids, drivers, and gardeners.

In the languid town of Beasu in the Viqueque district, a mooted site of a future LNG liquefaction plant, I stopped to catch some shade in the shadows of the quaint Portuguese-era church. I had been wandering around the town for too long in the broiling heat, and needed some time to cool down. I could see why the town was called 'Dog Water', named apparently for a time when someone saw a canine rolling in the sea to escape the clammy heat. An old sacristan from the church asked me what I was doing, and I explained that I was trying to see for myself what the current reality was like in towns that the government promised to transform into 'petro-cities'. According to the government's plan, this sleepy hamlet would metamorphose into a resource hub, but I saw little evidence of this underway, beyond a piece of empty land that was fenced off with metal sheets that were too hot to touch in the afternoon heat. The prime minister had recently been in Beasu as part of his tour spruiking the Strategic Development Plan, but my companion either did not believe or could not conceive of all the promises he heard. He was not interested in high-powered talk about international air links or a hyper-fast Internet. He did not have the money for a plane fare or a computer to access the web. He was more concerned by the absence of basic necessities than with the realisation of grand dreams. There was just six hours of electricity a day, no piped water, the sanitation was poor, and sometimes the roads were barely passable. As in many parts of the southern coast, I felt little sense that there was even a state in existence. 'Our politicians go to Dili and forget us. We can only blame ourselves now,' the sacristan said forlornly.

Perhaps his pessimism was further explained by the fact that he'd heard it all before. This was not the first time that his little town had been the centre of what political scientists would call a 'resources bubble'. In the late 1950s and early 1960s, Beasu was one of the towns on the southern coast that had been home to geologists, seismologists, drillers, helicopter pilots, and sea captains who came from as far away as Texas to prospect for liquid gold. The old man would have been a young boy when the prospectors came, flown in for their twenty-eight-day shifts not dissimilar to those which their successors are doing now on gas and oil rigs out in the Timor sea. They arrived flushed with expectation. With giddy anticipation, one oilman told the Australian papers in the early 1960s that Timor was, 'the biggest oil concession I had ever seen', and there was a rush of interest in Portuguese Timor.

The English anthropologist Margaret King, who wrote a joyously prim travelogue about her visit to the island in the early

1960s, flew from Darwin to Baucau with some of the men *en route* to Beasu. She wrote scoldingly about how much drunken noise they made in her hotel during the first night of her stay, and she revelled in their hangovers the next morning. 'My companions at breakfast were singularly changed from the night before — silent now, ashen-faced, hollow-eyed and distinctly "under the weather",' she gloated. Her book gives the impression that she probably would have been tucked up in her hotel bed with a cup of cocoa no later than nine o'clock.

The drunken carousing of the oilmen in Baucau may well have been their last fun for a while. The men lived in *palapa* huts that were like furnaces during the day and were still too warm at night to allow them to enjoy a restful sleep. Mosquitoes nipped at them constantly. The company even shipped an 18-foot python from Australia to eat the plague of rats that infested their accommodation. It was a far cry from the gilded conditions of present-day oil workers. The operation's communications base was a thatched hut manned by Celestino dos Anjos. He had worked with the Australian army during the Second World War, and the ghosts of that occupation haunted their headquarters. The operation was based beside a large tree that had been used by the Japanese to hang Timorese supporters of the Australian army. In the course of its explorations, the oil company would discover many hundreds of skeletons.

The men came there because they heard the stories of spontaneous seepages of oil from the ground, hot sands, and places where flames flickered up from the ground — all potential evidence of greater reserves onshore and just offshore. When the crews arrived they heard stories that, during the Second World War, the Japanese had fuelled their trucks and cars simply by digging pits into the ground and scooping out the oil in buckets. The annual shareholder report of the Timor Oil company in 1960 said that the oil-bearing potential of the area was apparent 'even to the layman', and many Australians invested large sums in successive share issues of the company, gambling that the excited words of its directors would come true. Shares rocketed with news of every supposedly lucrative breakthrough, and each oilman who came back through Darwin gushed to the local newspaper, raising hopes still further. Some of their appraisals, however, seemed better informed than others. Kevin Sherlock had meticulously clipped each article. One of the boosters, the skipper of the barge that transported the drilling equipment from northern Australia to southern Timor, based his confidence of a big find solely on his unbreakable belief that there was a connection between monkeys living nearby and the presence of oil.

These confident reports led other companies to extend their own searches from onshore to offshore prospecting. In both Viqueque and down the coast in Suai, the crews drilled down to nearly 1,500 metres in the hope of finding the oil that they were convinced was underneath. It was tough work; the rains that lashed the southern coast meant work was suspended for weeks at a time. Successive holes collapsed because the soil was too muddy to support the drills.

Jose Masceranas worked on a bore site. He was a teenage mechanic in Viqueque town, and had done such a thorough job fixing one of the foreigner's cars that they had hired him on the spot. He sailed to Darwin with the company's boat, and remembers marvelling at the size and wide-open spaces of Australia. The arrival was news enough to warrant a picture-feature in the *Northern Territory News*, which meant it gained a place in Kevin's archive. The journalist who wrote up the story must have reached for his phrasebook of hoary stereotypes to describe the Timorese newcomers as 'likeable, pint-sized natives' who were frightened of motorcars.

Nearly fifty years on, Jose was one of only two local men still alive who had worked for Timor Oil. The other was Abilio da Silva, a stoker who had worked on the boats that went between the various drill sites. Both were now in their seventies, and living lives that were far from wealthy. Jose spent his days sitting in a hut watching the world go by, and was by now a bit unsteady. This was not just due to old age and the effects of a recent stroke; his cousin said that something traumatic had happened during the Indonesian times that reduced this body of once-tight sinew to decrepitude. Abilio, a man with a full head of snowy white hair, had fared somewhat better, and still worked each day in the fields near his home.

They both remembered the great excitement when foreigners arrived unannounced one day. Previously, the only foreigners they had ever met were the Portuguese administrators. Now, planes and helicopters flew in and out of Viqueque, disgorging men who spoke unintelligible languages and who were much louder than the Timorese around them. Jose learned some English, which meant that he was very useful as an interpreter; he spoke just a little now, but you could hear a faint Australian accent when he said, 'Good morning'. Abilio found English difficult, and I asked him how he communicated. By way of explanation, he pointed to my companion's packet of cigarettes, and made a repeated pushing motion of his thumb. 'That's how we communicated,' he said. It may have been pretty easy to ask for a smoke, but much more difficult to transfer complex instructions, I thought.

The spending boom in Dili had yet to trickle down many benefits to either man or their families. They received their pensions, but their complaints echoed that of the sacristan: they still needed to walk to fetch water, and did not have access to clean toilets. The

THE LURE OF EASY MONEY 181

road, built by the Japanese during the war, was still not sealed, and it was pocked with large holes. 'All the money goes into politicians' pockets and not down to the people,' one of the old men said. 'There's lots of promises.' The huts that I slept in on the trip were not very different from those the oilmen had described fifty years earlier. The schools are still without desks and paper, and qualified teachers. Many children in Viqueque suffer from malnutrition, diarrhoea, and malaria. They lived in a world far away from the honeydew dreams of the development plan and the blandishments about economic growth.

Apart from the excitement at the beginning of the oil find, the two old men also remembered the increased frustration of their colleagues as the years went on and no big commercial discoveries were made. After a few years, the company closed over the holes and moved on, selling the concession to another company called Woodside that had, a decade previously, begun to search in an area fifty miles off the Timorese coast that was in a geographic no-man's-land. No one knew whether the sea belonged to Portuguese Timor or Australia. The *Northern Territory News* wrote that, 'Nobody would worry about the actual granting of the permit to prospect but the situation might be radically different if the company struck oil.'

How prescient the newspaper was. The oil that the company discovered in the Timor Sea still complicates relations between Australia and Timor-Leste. The prospecting ships were searching for unusual patterns of sediment on the seabed that indicated there were reserves underneath. It is an inexact business, and for months they traversed these stretches of sea and found nothing. Then, one day in 1974, they hit it lucky and discovered a large gas field between Australia and Portuguese Timor, closer to the latter than the former. They gave their new find the name 'Greater Sunrise', apparently after the blood-orange first light of morning.

There is still nothing that marks the Greater Sunrise field as being different from any other part in the Timor Sea. There are no platforms, no derricks, no workers, no helicopters, and no maritime guards. Not a cubic inch of gas has yet been drawn commercially from the seabed since its discovery nearly forty years ago. These are the grey, choppy, and swirling waters that have been the subject of countless bitter arguments and bad blood between Australia and its northern neighbour. The deeds that were done over the oil and gas in the sea continue to curse relations between the two nations. Australia is Timor-Leste's largest donor, but no amount of aid donations can compensate for past actions. Like many things in Timor-Leste, the future is the son of the past. Australia is still trying to erase the sins it committed when it made a grab for the oil.

The problems began in the early 1970s when Australia and Indonesia negotiated the seabed boundaries between the two nations. Portugal declined to be involved in the negotiations, meaning that the other two countries could not complete the boundary line between Portuguese Timor and Australia. This created the geographical no-man's-land known as the 'Timor Gap'.

The reserves were big enough to justify an act of appalling political expediency that cost thousands of lives. Australia knew that an Indonesian invasion was imminent, and even listened in to the shootings in Dili on invasion day. Canberra gave the diplomatic equivalent of a nod and a wink to the military takeover. Cold war concerns were also likely to have played a role, possibly not helped by the Che Guevara fashion styles popular in Timor at the time. Australia's relationship with Indonesia was too strategically important and too financially lucrative for them to raise an objection; oil and gas reserves seemed more important to lobby for than an independent Timor. 'The present gap in the agreed seabed border ... could be much more readily negotiated with Indonesia ... than with Portugal or an independent Portuguese Timor. I know I am recommending a pragmatic rather than a principled stand but that is what national interest and foreign policy is all about,' sniffed Richard Woolcott. He was the Australian ambassador to Indonesia, and sent this in a cable back to Canberra in August 1975, months before Indonesia invaded Timor-Leste. To put it in a more undiplomatic way, he was recommending that Australia allow the Indonesians to annex Timor-Leste.

In 1978, Australia was the first country to formally recognise the Indonesian annexation of Timor. Although the countries did not agree on the boundaries to close the Timor Gap, they reached an arrangement to split the oil revenues. Ten years afterwards, the foreign ministers, Gareth Evans of Australia and Ali Alatas of Indonesia, flew over the Timor Sea in a government jet to toast the deal. With their champagne glasses clinking, neither side disturbed the bonhomie by mentioning that Timor-Leste had been essentially erased from the map. Clearly, neither expected to see its status restored. The photo of Australia's then foreign minister having a celebratory drink in the plane was used regularly in the Timorese media as a way of reminding the Australians of a past they'd have preferred to forget.

Decades later, the return of Timor-Leste from the graveyard of short-lived nations presented problems for Australia on the previously settled matter of resources. Now Australia would need to negotiate maritime boundaries with the new state. It turned out to be an acrimonious negotiation. Each bureaucratic twist and spiteful turn in the proceedings is recounted in *Shakedown*, Paul Cleary's readable blow-by-blow account of the fractious diplomacy between the two neighbours. Cleary is an Australian, but does not hold back in his account of his country's bullying and mean-spirited tactics, which ranged from withdrawing from international arbitration to an odd story about how a night of cocktails at a bijoux beachside restaurant in Dili was enlivened by the Australian ambassador bellowing upbraids at international advisers working with the Timorese government.

When Cleary wrote his final chapter, he might have thought that would be the end of the saga. Timor-Leste and Australia signed the Treaty on Certain Maritime Arrangements in the Timor Sea, which split the upstream revenues of Greater Sunrise between the two countries on a 50/50 basis. The decision as to where the pipeline would go devolved to Woodside and partners, who would make the decision based on what would maximise earnings for the oil companies. The Timorese parliament approved the treaty, and the then president, Xanana Gusmao, signed the treaty into law.

That, you might have thought, would have been that. And yet so much has happened since then that there is probably another book's worth of material for Cleary, should he choose to write a sequel. In 2010, Woodside suggested that a floating platform would be the best option, and the Timorese government, led by the very man who had signed the treaty into law, angrily rejected this on the grounds that, if Darwin had one plant processing gas from the shared fields, Timor should have the next one. The government cited numerous studies it had commissioned, which reported that this was the most commercially viable option, but refused to release them to enable other parties to compare and contrast the conclusions.

The government dug in further: it would not approve any development plan unless it included a pipeline to Timor-Leste and an LNG plant on the south coast. It refused to negotiate, instead sending out bombastic press releases underlining its rejections.

The strategy appeared to be to wear all parties down by engaging in a war of attrition. 'The lack of professionalism, transparency and attempts to misguide the process will not be accepted by our Government and our people,' thundered one press release, which listed a number 'for further inquiries' of a phone that was always switched off. The caustic nationalistic bromides may well have been written over a cappuccino in Sydney.

The pinnacle of high farce was a multi-billion-dollar game of pass-the-parcel over the development plan. When Woodside attempted to deliver its plan for the floating LNG plant to the Timorese regulator, the regulator refused to accept the folder, and so Woodside representatives left it on a desk on the way out. A security guard immediately ran out to their car and tried to push it through the driver's window — thus creating a new saga about whether the plan had been lodged with the regulator or not. Jose Belo of *Tempo Semanal* captured the antics on video and posted them immediately on YouTube.

The oil and gas saga is about more than cash and industrial development. To put it one way, it is about the desire to create a real petro-state, complete with a refinery and infrastructure, rather than a nominal one that just receives payments into its bank account. To put it another way, it is about national sovereignty and pride, and a determination to defend the resources that were found near the huts where Jose and Abilio live.

The army's mission is now to protect the riches of the sea, even though its patrol boats only have enough fuel reserves for a one-way journey to the south coast. The difficulty, of course, is that with so much focus still on the destination of the pipeline, less attention is devoted to what is important — namely, ensuring that the money that is coming in, and will continue to do so in the future, will be spent wisely. There is also little attention devoted to whether there will be sufficient investment in education, health, planning, and infrastructure to reap the true benefits of the revenues. It is easier to focus attention on the issue of building a pipeline than it is on building the sort of state that is envisaged in the constitution, not to mention building an economy that can sustain the people of Timor-Leste after the oil runs out.

The organisation that has worked most closely on this issue is known colloquially as *La'o Hamutuk* (Walking Together), a think tank run by a collection of national and international activists and local researchers. The collective used to be located in the leafy Dili suburb of Farol, in a building that was formerly the home of Portuguese governors, Indonesian consuls, and senior UN administrators, and is now home to members of the Timorese political elite. In 2011, *La'o Hamutuk* moved because, despite years of trying, it could not negotiate a long-term lease with the government.

Its new office is just around the corner from the magnificently refurbished Cathedral of the Immaculate Conception, a show project that cost over US$20 million — much of which was public oil money contributed by the Timor-Leste government's 'Civil Society Fund'. On the walls of the new office there is a picture of Gareth Evans toasting his Indonesian counterpart over the Timor Sea, and also one from 2004 of Prime Minister Gusmao with his arms around Indonesia's General Wiranto, who had recently been indicted for crimes against humanity committed when he headed the Indonesian military in 1999.

The Timorese government seems more prepared to forgive and forget the behaviour of its counterparts in Jakarta than those in Canberra. Perhaps it is because they know only too well what the Indonesian government is capable of, and that Australian ambassadors will be more inclined than their counterparts in Jakarta to sit and take the verbal punches without rebukes or threats.

I found *La'o Hamutuk* a salving place to visit. It was one of only a few offices in Dili — government or international — where Facebook or solitaire is not hastily minimised on the office computer screens as one walks in. Unlike many government (and international) offices, people arrive early and leave late. And, even more amazingly in a land of extremely differentiated wages, the local and international staffs are paid the same salaries, and work with the same terms and conditions. The NGO is widely respected, mainly for the quality of its information, research, analysis, and comment on socio-economic issues, and many times it is the only organisation providing written comments on important issues such as the Petroleum Fund and the state budget. Many of the embassies of countries that once cold-shouldered the notion of Timorese independence now rely heavily for their information on the free analysis of these former activists.

Probably the most public face of the collective is an ex-software engineer from New York called Charlie Scheiner, who, in my view, is probably among the most important and influential of all *malae* in Timor. He has dedicated the best part of his adult life to campaigning for an end to Indonesian occupation and the restoration of Timorese independence, and has lived in Dili for most of the last decade. Charlie is agreeably prickly and argumentative, like a dog with a bone; occasionally, he would politely point out the darker elements in the history between the two neighbours, but his candour is not reserved for the international set alone. He does not shy from pointing out to the Timorese government that the optimism brought on by the resource boom belies more fundamental and endemic structural problems. He seems to pop up at almost every meeting and, through the length of his tenure and his continuing demonstrations of usefulness, is now more integral than most in a culture that emphasises and confers privileges based on personal familiarity. In 2012, he was awarded the 'Order of Timor-Leste', one of the country's highest honours.

I have a huge amount of time for the man. Temperamentally, we're very different, but when I'm in my early sixties I'd love to have the zeal and passion of Charlie Scheiner to argue for what is right, although I'm not sure I'd look as good with his bushy beard.

La'o Hamutuk was a pleasant environment to meet Scheiner in, but my talk with him and Juvinal Dias, a young researcher who wore a yellow T-shirt with the slogan 'Best to keep the oil in the ground', was sobering. They bombarded me with depressing facts, each one either based on a detailed reading of public documents or coaxed out of knowledgeable people who have chosen not to put what they know in official documents. Charlie and Juvinal have come to the conclusion that Timor-Leste is a resource state without many resources. Yes, the government's budget is dependent on oil and gas, but that it not necessarily an indication of deep reserves. It merely emphasises how little else there is to rely on to drive the economy. Timor-Leste's proven reserves are, in fact, quite low. The new nation is currently the most resource-revenue-dependent country in the world, but the reserves will provide an income of less than $2 per person per day for the next few decades — hardly enough for any ordinary person to be considered a 'lucky winner'. And the reserves will probably run out before today's babies finish high school: given the current political disagreements over the Greater Sunrise field, Timor's known reserves are projected to run out by 2024.

According to the collective's analysis, the government's decisions to ignore, neglect, and downplay the development of non-oil sectors of the economy looks more and more rickety and short-term — especially given an expanding population, and more and more people looking to enter the workplace. They see this as particularly depressing, given the postwar baby boom (there are twice as many children aged 0–9 as people aged 20–29) and the lack of decent primary education for most of them. Big spending is leading to high levels of inflation, which hits the poor the hardest. Timor-Leste is not going to be the Qatar of South-East Asia; but if it keeps on spending at its currently prodigious rate, it may turn out to be the next Nauru. That tiny atoll nation in the middle of the Pacific Ocean had one of the highest per-capita incomes in the world in the 1980s from exporting its phosphate; now, with the resources gone, it has one of the lowest. The money was squandered on ill-advised property deals and a spending spree that went on far too long.

Perhaps the biggest risk is that, in spending big now, the wealth will all be gone without having laid the groundwork for an economy that can support people's lives in the future. Petroleum-derived wealth is the only thing that can allow Timor-Leste to escape permanent poverty. If it's wasted, there's no fallback plan. Currently, the government is dipping into the capital of the Petroleum Fund, originally set up to steward the windfall for future generations, and has been doing so since 2009. By 2012, Timor-Leste had the second-fastest-growing state budget in the world. It is also borrowing money from abroad. The argument in favour of this approach is easy to make: as government advisers had told me, the small nation's straits are so dire that the money is needed to kick-start the development process, and not let it chug along. But the results, so far, are not encouraging. The Petroleum Fund Law was revised in September 2011 to enable more risky, high-return investments, in the hope of increasing the fund's returns. But, as most stockmarket punters know, betting on longer-shot equities does not always work. Two hundred million dollars has been allocated to an investment company that has proposed investments which sound flashy and questionable, at best. One of their proposals is for a high-quality shopping centre ready to offer 'the lowest prices in the region'. Is this really possible in one of the most expensive countries in Asia? Charlie and Juvinal feared that the Anti-Corruption Commission was not sufficiently empowered to investigate those with the stench of corruption about their person. Many government officials with responsibilities for the pots of money at their disposal are in over their heads, and not susceptible to advice. Ideas about what to do with the funds are too often little more than dreams. By 2014, the government will be spending more in oil money than it is getting in revenue. According to Charlie and Juvinal, this is financial madness.

The NGO's call for prudence is indubitably right, but it is an unpalatable message in this land of suddenly easy money, especially when many seem to be benefitting from the largesse — from the multi-million-dollar contractor with his house in Bali, to the gap-toothed old man who uses the government's regular thirty-dollar payment to eke out another month. In a country as poor as Timor-Leste, it is understandably hard for many Timorese to get too worked up about the problems that come with having money. For most Timorese, getting a good house and a motorbike are much more pressing matters than adhering to international best practice. It is also the sort of strategy that wins elections for political parties. There are strong political and personal incentives in the here-and-now to follow what may not be the most economically prudent course of action. One day, though, in the not-too-distant future, a prime minister may come to check the state accounts, only to find that there is no money in the bank — or, worse, billions of dollars of unrepayable debt on the balance sheets.

Chapter Nine

The Tropical Bakery School of International Capacity-Building

Before the UN left, the Tropical Bakery used to be the perfect place to discuss local politics, unencumbered by the risk that one might run into an actual Timorese person. The only Timorese around were the waitresses, ferrying $2.50 lattes to *malae* in a city where, despite the sudden wealth, most scraped by on less than that amount in a day. The Tropical was a stone's throw from the United Nations compound, and it often seemed to serve as the organisation's living room. It was an easy place to spot who else was skiving off from work (or was otherwise in a serious meeting outside the office). The restaurant also served as a base camp for the many people who seemed to be conducting research about Timor-Leste, albeit in probably one of the most culturally unrepresentative places in the country. During the busy lunchtime shift, there would be, at a bare minimum, the recipients of two million dollars' worth of international adviser salaries inspecting the yellow menus that were getting a bit tatty through over-perusal. There was something truly, appallingly, wonderful about the place. Where else could one have seen self-described experts on the justice system struggle to convey accurately a request for ketchup to the waiting staff, and then return without any sense of irony to a discussion of the 'learning challenges' faced by Timorese lawyers?

My office was directly across the road, and I used to spend an unholy amount of time in the Tropical. I'd rib the place and its po-faced denizens frequently; but, as my wife never tired of teasing me, I was magnetically drawn there almost every day. I came up with a whole host of reasons to justify why I spent so much time there, but none of them convinced either of us. I guess I have to admit that I felt at home there, opining authoritatively about things that, in truth, I knew precious little about. The ham-and-cheese croissants were also to die for, although the coffee didn't live up to their standard.

One day, I was having lunch with a high-level UN functionary. As we finished our salmon fettuccine, he made one of the two most profound statements I had heard in the four years I'd spent in Timor-Leste. Giving voice to a frustration never hinted at in the official cables he sent back to New York, he threw up his arms in frustration and said, 'If we [the United Nations] can't be successful here, in this tiny place with not much crime and a relatively decent political leadership, where can we be successful?' He was right. That there seem to be such minimal dividends for the UN's labours in this relatively enabling and financially well-supported setting augurs poorly for other, much more malign, environments. If there can't be effective international assistance here, what hope is there for efforts in places such as Afghanistan, the Democratic Republic of Congo, or South Sudan? His question holds true, not just for the work of the United Nations, but for all aid donors working in states emerging from conflict.

The problem, however, was that what happened in the Tropical stayed in the Tropical. There was never as much candour, let alone action, over the need to change the state of affairs after the lunch tab was settled. In leaden, bureaucratic prose, meetings attended would be ballyhooed; committees formed and talked up; statements lauded; and the crushing bureaucratic work environment ignored. Spin and an almost congenital need to report unalloyed success complicated efforts to genuinely evaluate the activities of the international community. To some extent, this is understandable in the short term, but it has bruising implications for the manner in which assistance is assessed in the longer term. Take, for example, the reporting from almost all agencies prior to the 2006 crisis. It was all sunny news, with not a mention of dark clouds looming large on the horizon.

Almost all expats in Timor-Leste were there to help, but it was an open question as to whether their efforts were constructive or not. More than ten years after the arrival of an alphabet soup of UN agencies, the European Union, aid programs run by countries such as Australia and Portugal, and a cavalcade of NGOs, the results are mixed. Although Timor-Leste receives among the highest per-capita allocations of aid in the world, it is hard to believe that much of it has made a real difference to ordinary people's lives. Malnourishment levels in the population remain higher than that of sub-Saharan Africa, according to AusAid, Timor-Leste's biggest donor. According to UNDP figures released in 2013, 49.9 per cent of Timorese live below the poverty line, which is US$0.88 a day.

These statistics are no secret. They glare accusingly from the glossy brochures produced by aid agencies, which can be found in embassy waiting rooms and the offices of international organisations. They are, no doubt, slipped into briefing packs for dignitaries to read on the plane-ride over. This really makes one wonder why many of the suggestions that they then announce seem, oftentimes, so utterly divorced from the realities of the villages and towns that they fly over on their approach into Dili airport. This dissonance isn't peculiar to Timor-Leste. Colleagues and friends in the development industry around the world all point to the way that development is often about what foreigners think the locals should have, rather than being based on asking local people what they need and what would fit in with the local environment.

A few of the schemes and programs proposed by the international community have the air of something dreamed up between take-off and landing. Whether it was the Angolan delegation promising a direct air link between Luanda and Dili, the Polish ambassador suggesting naval assistance, the Austrians proposing to set up a tenor choir, or the Nigerian delegate at the annual donors' meeting offering his country up as a 'model' of clean government, no claim seemed too outlandish or inapt not to be sincerely offered by the earnest national representative sweating in the humid heat. Even Jackie Chan showed up one day, with a few well-timed high roundhouse kicks for the cameras, delivering his message to Timorese youth to stay away from martial-arts gangs. Ireland also got in on the act, sending down a 'Special Envoy on Conflict Resolution' to share the lessons of Northern Ireland that the Timorese didn't ask for and more or less politely ignored for several years. There seemed to be at least two visits a week from ministers and secretaries of state flying a national flag and touting some half-baked scheme.

The centrepiece of many visits is the signing of a memorandum of understanding (MoU), known as an 'announceable' in diplomatic and political circles. Such a document has as much legal validity as a gentleman's agreement, but is a tried-and-tested means of demonstrating progress, as well as filing a press release justifying the trip and providing a photo opportunity. By my count, Timor-Leste signed a grand total of forty-one different accords on suitably vague topics in the first half of 2011. The president signed a MoU with Angola on the defence and communications sector (with, sadly, no mention of the long-touted air link), and agreements were reached with countries on every continent. These included 'energy policy' with Portugal; 'economic co-operation' with Sao Tome and Principe; 'decentralisation', 'public works', and 'diplomatic education' with Indonesia (along with two separate agreements on 'health' that seem to contradict each other); and 'economic development' with Ireland, a country that knows only too well the perils that come with getting rich quickly.

God knows what happens to these MoUs afterwards; there is no central repository for them, and many can't be found. It is hard to know who signed what, what the follow-up was or might have been, and how subsequent MoUs sit with previous announcements. Donors rarely seem to cross-reference how an MoU interacts with their own programs. As many are written in verbose English or Portuguese, civil servants are rarely able to read the documents — or know what to do with them. Perhaps this explains why programs so triumphantly heralded at the time often get quickly forgotten. I can't recall a political development during which anyone referred to a previous MoU subsequent to the ink drying — pretty poor value for all those business-class air tickets. (The Irish foreign minister's two-day trip to Timor-Leste in 2008 cost Irish taxpayers nearly half a million dollars alone. In the dying days of the Celtic Tiger, the minister and his entourage flew from Dublin in the official government jet.)

The staff of countries represented within Timor-Leste hawk their pet projects, irrespective of whether or not they make sense or would ever work in their own countries. The only country that didn't seem to be out and about being a craven self-promoter was China, which was much happier to let the large buildings they gave the Timorese government speak for themselves. The Chinese built the new presidential palace, the Defence headquarters, and the Foreign Affairs building (complete with Dili's first elevator). I was told by many authoritative sources (that is, those who had heard the rumour just before I did) that the inner walls of each building might not necessarily be filled just with concrete. No one really seemed to mind.

Irrespective of the topic, what unites many MoUs, country strategies, programs, projects, action plans, work plans, and frameworks is an attempt to impose some sort of neat, practical order on a social and political system that is more complex and personality-based than most forms of human endeavour. Organisations cling to plans like comfort blankets. It doesn't seem to matter whether or not they are useful or even used in the course of day-to-day life. The mere fact of the existence of a plan seems to be its prime purpose.

A colleague of mine called Ray Murray, who had been working on police development since 2003, had taken to keeping all the plans he'd acquired over the years. The legs of his desk sagged under their weight. Each plan had a name that sounded as if it had been randomly thrown up by a word-generating machine on a bureaucratic cycle. The plans bore serious titles such as Sector Investment Program, Sector Expenditure Program, Institutional Capacity Building Committee, and Joint Assessment Mission. They were all in English and, as he said, not a single one had been read by anyone in the government. There are page after page of matrixes and checklists of documents, policies, and procedures that only a brave soul would be likely to plough through, with only the occasional piece of creative writing buried within the text as an oasis of reprieve. One meeting in 2003, in which the Timorese prime minister arrived unannounced to angrily denounce the

UN's efforts as a sham, was apparently written up internally as: 'The meeting was further enhanced by the presence of the Prime Minister, who provided insightful comments.' All of these 'reform processes' seemed to 'progress' in a similar arc: there was the initial announcement; a set-piece meeting rich in pledges as to how this effort would be different from the others; the creation of working groups; the development of a 'technical framework matrix'; the arrival of new staff; a revision of the 'technical framework matrix'; the reality of working groups failing to work; some more meetings; a report drafted in English and marked 'joint report'; less regular meetings; and, finally, a glowing self-evaluation report. A few months and years later, the only evidence that any of this ever took place was to be found in the weathered pages on Ray's desk.

When I arrived in Timor-Leste in 2007, the talk at the Tropical was of a new initiative with a catchy title: 'The Triple-R Plans for Police Development'. The 'Triple-R' stood for 'Reform, Restructuring and Rebuilding', and the basic idea behind it could not be faulted. The United Nations had returned to Timor-Leste the previous year, following the implosion of the police force, and its aim was to sharpen the areas of focus needed to rebuild the institution. This was to be accomplished through the Timorese police and the UN working jointly on a plan and then implementing it together. What could possibly go wrong? Regrettably, the good intentions withered quickly. The Timorese police frequently didn't show up to meetings in which the dominant language was English, and the drafts were being tweaked so often that translators could not keep up. The task fell to a group of United Nations police officers who were relatively fresh off the plane, rather than to anyone on the ground who happened to know anything in detail about the subject or the country. The pressure to produce a plan was intense, in order to report forward progress to the Security Council.

The result was a total and unmitigated mess. Removed from day-to-day realities in their air-conditioned offices at UN headquarters in Dili, the assembled officers produced a three-hundred-page thumper of a document that contained inaccuracies on almost every page. Some of its unacknowledged pilfering would no doubt have interested the World Intellectual Property Organisation. I once ran the document through plagiarism software: my computer nearly melted down through over-exertion, so many different (and unacknowledged) copy-and-pastes did it discover, ranging from the preface to a US medical school textbook to the Bible itself. And, of course, it was never translated into a language that the Timorese police could read. 'Have you ever read this document?' asked a senior (English-speaking) Timorese official to me one day, adding, 'I've meant to, but it is just *soooo* long.'

The United Nations is like a down-on-his-luck Las Vegas gambler convinced that if he plays the same hand again and again, he'll eventually win. Undaunted by past failures, the default strategy is always to develop more plans in English that are equally wordy and bureaucratic. In 2012, and a few years after the Triple-R catastrophe, the United Nations produced another proposal called the 'Joint Development Plan' that had apparently been agreed to in 'working groups', but which was so well written in bureaucratic English that suspicious souls would think it had been produced on a word processor inside the United Nations compound. It was a 'capacity-building program for the national police, focusing on legislation, training, administration, discipline and operations'. Even accepting the document at face value, it begged the obvious question as to why the UN was only getting around to doing this now, after having been in the country for more than ten years. Presumably, the answer was that everyone had been too busy attending workshops and writing plans to do any work. I was told that the only 'committee' which met in any way regularly was the one that discussed the gifting of assets.

The aim of many plans of the United Nations and others — including the program that I worked on — is to build something that cannot be seen and is hard to quantify, but which is considered very important: 'capacity'. Millions of dollars are spent each year trying to 'build the capacity' of Timorese police, lawyers, prosecutors, public servants, customs officials, and a range of others. Some of the aims of these projects are so vague that it would be hard for anyone to verify whether they have been successful or not. Trying to define the point of many projects in the thirty-eight-page, small-type-size, single-spaced Multi-Donor Assistance form is challenging. The formally expected outcomes of two Portuguese projects called 'Institutional capacity building to the President (sic) office' and 'Institutional capacity building to the Ministry of Foreign Affairs Office' are 'President Office capacitated' and 'Ministry of Foreign Affairs capacitated'. One could charitably put this vagueness down to a poor translation, but those written by native English speakers are hardly any clearer. Among the modest goals of the Inclusive Finance for Underserved Economy Program, implemented by UNDP policy development, is 'Livelihood improved and social stability' and 'Strategic coordination to enhance the enabling environment'. If anyone knows what this means, they deserve the funds on offer.

Perhaps not entirely coincidentally, most of the money does not go to Timor-Leste, but boomerangs back into the capacity-builder's bank account. The Dili-based NGO *La'o Hamutuk* estimates that around 90 per cent of development assistance never reaches the country, being mostly spent on salaries, overseas procurement, imported supplies, and overseas costs.

Being such an expensive business, you'd think that there would be clear definitions of the most critical objective of all. Not so. I never got an entirely convincing answer from anyone as to what 'capacity-building' meant. The more people I asked to explain the term, the more I got the sense that no one could define it. 'Just go out and develop some ideas, but don't rush it,' said one expert — which seemed to be heard by the staff as an injunction to sit in coffee shops.

The logic of most of the 'capacity-building' projects seems to run thus: institution X is lacking in policy and processes, which means that it isn't working as well as it should (which translates as 'the way that foreigners would like it to work'). Accordingly, 'experts' in this particular field need to be brought in, in order to build up the 'capacity' of individuals to help them run their affairs for themselves. But there are real, glaring problems with this idea. As I noted in earlier chapters, the basic problem of inaccessible language dooms many efforts. A *malae* who went up to a government office to provide (much-needed) file-management assistance was surprised to find that no one spoke English; the individual never pursued the matter. I once attended a meeting on Timorese national-security policy development, where we discussed the difference between 'progress' and 'process'. A 'senior adviser' in the 'security sector' who had been in Timor-Leste since the arrival of the United Nations led the conversation. He loved nothing more than displaying his verbal dexterity and knowledge of the country, casually disclosing his close relationship with 'Prime Minister Xanana'. I was enjoying his sophomoric presentation so much that I forgot the conversation was taking place entirely in English. 'What do these words mean?' whispered my Timorese colleague. When I asked the UN man to translate what he'd said, he suddenly became very coy.

For some, there was the challenge of dealing with people from a culture very different from their own. I sometimes got the impression that certain people would do anything but sit down and spend time with their Timorese colleagues during office hours. I heard numerous reasons for this over the years, ranging from the precious (inadequate Internet speed) and the procedural (no key cut) to the downright ineffable (insufficiently large desk). At its core, I think that many were more comfortable grousing over coffee with their own cultural group (whether they were Australians, Portuguese, New Zealanders, or whatever) than in making the effort to interact with others.

None of what I've written so far would be particularly new to the Dili lunch set, or indeed to anyone who works in a peacekeeping mission or aid organisation. Much of the chat among foreigners in coffee shops is gallows talk about how whatever program they are working on is not achieving its stated aims. 'The Timorese just don't seem that interested,' they say, engaging in the verbal equivalent of a long shake of the head. Useless colleagues are a standby topic when there is a gap in the conversation; verbally flaying the efforts of others accompanies most lunchtime tête-à-têtes. Their laments are little different from those of the Portuguese in Dili more than one hundred years previously. But then a curious thing happens once the plates and coffee cups are cleared away: the flayers return to their cubicles, and devise reports of success and progress for their respective headquarters, irrespective of whether or not what is reported accords with what is happening. Failures or hiatuses — natural occurrences in any endeavour, but especially in an unstable operating context — are rarely mentioned in bureaucratic reporting. Drafts are carefully edited to please the bosses back at headquarters, a place that staffers casually refer to by the name of the city in which it's situated, rather than by the name of the organisation itself. ('We need to send back this info in the "weekly" to Canberra'; 'New York is looking for this information ASAP'.)

I did see a few good initiatives that had been well thought through and delivered by dedicated staff when I was in Timor-Leste. When I worked for an Australian government police program, I saw programs delivered in criminal investigations that were nothing short of outstanding. The teachers were well versed, the classes were lively, and the students were enthusiastic and received more from it than the standard certificate. The students were tested at the beginning and end of the courses in order to discern if they were actually learning anything. I also saw dedicated aid workers burrowing away to good effect in all sorts of different sectors. Sanitation was improved, and crops produced higher yields, because of the assistance they provided. The problem, however, is that if every initiative is written up as a triumph of perspicacious design and wise implementation, it is hard to know the difference between a dud and a success. This is disingenuous, and prevents any honest reflections about what is happening. The net effect of ever-sunny reporting is that after a while only the naïve believe what any institution has to say.

The many critical academic reports published on the efforts of international organisations in Timor-Leste appear to have made not a whit of difference. Instead, when an adverse report was sent out over the East Timor and Indonesia Action Network list-serve, members of those organisations that had not been focused upon would gloat about the identified failures of the 'other side', rather than ask whether any of those failings also applied to them. I remember someone in one of the aid organisations telling me that staff members would focus on small factual errors or grammatical glitches within reports, seizing upon those as (thin) validations for why the report wasn't worth discussing. In any case, given the rapid turnover of staff within such contexts, many individuals had left Timor-Leste by the time an adverse assessment was published, allowing their replacements or former colleagues to treat any criticism as dealing with a sense of it being 'yesterday's problem'. Long before I came to Timor-Leste, I once co-wrote an article with an esteemed academic called Otwin Marenin that was half jokingly called 'Their Reports Are Not Read and Their Recommendations Are Resisted'. Our assertion may have been truer than we thought and feared.

'We've been here so long, so how come we've accomplished so little?' is another standard dirge of the international set, echoing again the tenor of letters and reports sent from Portuguese Timor in the last hundred years or more. There is a timeless quality to this sort of woebegone reflection, and it is certainly not confined to either this part of the tropics or this colonial heritage. Graham Greene's and George Orwell's characters, in their novels set in West Africa and Burma respectively, voiced similar-sounding gripes over gin and tonics, as did friends of mine who worked in Kabul and Kinshasa. The problem is that the grousing individuals fasten their criticism onto others and seldom reflect on how they themselves might do better.

'We' refers to the enterprise itself rather than to the individuals, many of whom stay for only a few months or, at best, a year or two. Accordingly, although it is factually accurate to say that 'the UN has been here for eleven years', it is more useful to say that there have been a series of much shorter engagements by different people, determined by their contracts and tenures. A one-year contract is lengthy in this business, but is little more than a grain of time, given that everyone seems to agree that they're engaged in a multi-generational endeavour.

The individuals' tenures tend to follow a similar trajectory: arrive; determine that one's predecessor hasn't done anything useful; attempt to find files; fail to find files; let it be known to all that there will be a 'new approach' markedly different from the previous lame effort; express initial enthusiasm; quickly find that it is not so easy after all; sink into despair; apply for a new job; count the days down until departure; make valedictory leaving speech; depart the country. The Portuguese governors followed a similar cycle. They arrived full of enthusiasm, determined to shake things up, only to leave worn out and beaten down a few years later. It seems that the system has always been premised on the curious notion that individuals sent for a relatively short period of time can somehow work well in a context that is politically, culturally, and linguistically alien to them.

Although other people are the subject of most lunchtime conversations in Dili, the capability of those sent there from overseas rarely gets an explicit mention in the ample literature on building states, beyond the use of stock phrases such as 'better training' and 'greater capability'. In reality, the politics within the international set have little to do with the grand policy schemes, technical measurements, and objective criteria held dear by many staff within the organisations. Their internal politics are every bit as premised on friendships, special understandings, extra-curricular relationships, and personalities as are the wider Timorese politics.

Inculcating the frequently advertised necessities of accountability is as difficult to do in the small international set as it is within the small Timorese elite. Dili is a small city in which people socialise with each other and constantly seem to know each other's business. This often makes it difficult to create information barriers within institutional structures. Accordingly, it is hard to separate and isolate the people who make accountability and oversight decisions from those who are the subject of those decisions.

The mid-life crisis that is the expat musical cover band What Lafaek was an example of the difficulty of even observing 'Do as I say' in such a small place. In English, the band's name means 'What Crocodile', which made no real sense until one of their followers told me it kind of sounds like 'What the Fuck', if you say it quickly enough. (I should probably have twigged when I saw a 'What Lafaek are you doing tonight?' sign behind the pictures of their fevered jamming on their promo posters.) The band comprised the manager of a 'justice facility' program; someone from the 'public sector capacity-building' program; a member of the donor institution (funding both programs); and the director of a UNDP justice-sector program who delivered her lines with a lusty gusto not seen since the heyday of Gloria Estefan and the Miami Sound Machine. The band played the occasional Saturday night 'fun-raising' [sic] gig down at Castaways — a sweaty expat bar on the Dili waterfront — where it rolled through a repertoire of soft-rock classics to their increasingly inebriated fans, many of whom seemed to have parked their cars badly outside. There was nothing untoward about what they did, apart from maiming the occasional Amy Winehouse song, but the ageing rockers showed the thin line between the personal and professional spheres in Dili. Come Monday morning, the male lead singer and the bass player needed to report progress to the place where the rhythm guitarist worked. Most anthropologists who come to Timor leave Dili relatively quickly and head for the hills; but if just one were to stay, he or she could come up with a fine ethnography of different local and cultural systems, and varied professions intermingling (or not) within the bars, coffee shops, and restaurants in the capital.

If I were to spend long enough in these sorts of places, I, too, could be deluded into thinking that international organisations were still in a position of influence in present-day Timor-Leste.

But it is not necessarily the norm for a *malae* to spend time with Timorese who he or she is meant to be working with. It is usual to meet someone else from another embassy, aid organisation, or NGO who is working on a similar issue — preferably over coffee or lunch — and always easier and less culturally awkward to find a fellow English-speaker to have chitchats with in a culturally familiar setting than to go beyond one's comfort zone. The natural extension of this would be the 'coordination' meeting, in which the assembled ranks would sit around, noting silently that they run a lot more smoothly without the Timorese around to complicate matters. This can then be reported back to headquarters as an example of 'donor coordination'. Press releases extolling the funding of a training program or the donation of a computer are intended to give the reader the impression that such items are essential to the smooth running of an office. The majority of reports, articles, and chapters published on Timor-Leste reinforce this *malae*-centric view of the world, reflective of the fact that a disproportionate number of interviews have been conducted with dejected staff in the Tropical Bakery and other hangouts.

This combination of long lunches, oversold claims, and relentlessly positive reporting serves to exaggerate the influence of the international community. It can be a personally rewarding strategy in the short-term, as accounts of meetings can be easily parlayed as a 'demonstrated ability to deliver results' in a job application or to get a promotion. However, over the longer term, it leads to seeing everything as the 'fault' of the internationals' presence — which often is not the case, owing to their relative *lack* of influence. Internationals are easy to blame when the balloon goes up, and it is difficult for them to use lack of influence as a defence, given that they regularly exaggerate their influence in florid achievement reports and budget submissions which imply that their particular program is the only thing standing between triumph and disaster in the new nation-state. However, the simple fact of the matter is that the Timorese government clearly feels it is time to run its own affairs, unbridled by foreigners poking their noses around and venturing their assessments of how the Timorese are doing it.

Flush with cash from oil and gas reserves, Timor-Leste no longer feels beholden to either the United Nations or to donor organisations for very much. Members of the government either cancel meetings at short notice or keep senior aid bureaucrats waiting for hours before they deign to see them — yet such powerful signs of lack of interest in their endeavours are not reported back to headquarters. I heard one story of the government's priggishness that illustrated the bind that organisations such as the United Nations are in. Tired of often being kept waiting for up to an hour in a steamy waiting room, only to find the meeting cancelled, one enterprising 'Special Assistant' adopted the approach of ringing up a moment before he hopped in the car to confirm that a scheduled meeting would take place. Following confirmation, he made the two-minute drive to the venue — only to find that the meeting had been cancelled 'at short notice'. This happened three weeks in a row. 'Why don't you report this petulance back to New York?' I asked casually, adopting the city-based shorthand of the international bureaucrat. 'I can't do that,' he groaned, as he hoisted himself on his own petard, 'because we've been spinning them good-news stories for the past few months.'

Similarly, supine scraping is the order of the day when the Timorese government criticises donors. In 2010, the prime minister livened up the opening to a donor's conference with a salvo of accusations about both Australia and the United States, and not a single official word was said by either country to rebut his accusations. A year later, he declared open season on the United Nations. Gumshoe journalist Jose Belo had acquired a copy of a PowerPoint presentation prepared by the UN for senior mission managers which implied that the prime minister was coveting ever more power for himself at the expense of parliament. Sensing a scoop, he had gleefully posted the slides on the Internet.

The prime minister was furious; he publicly dressed down UN staff, accusing them of hoping for misery in the country in order to prolong their tenure. He also got stuck into the Timorese staff working for the UN, saying they were afflicted with 'mental colonialism'. A few days later, the president weighed in to accuse the United Nations Integrated Mission in Timor-Leste (UNMIT) of not being fit to tie the prime minister's shoelaces, while my old friend Julio averred that the UN were about as useful as a 'blind cow', and accused members of its staff of working for national governments instead of for the common cause. The issue was front-page news for weeks in Dili, even knocking out of the headlines the case of a salacious sex video involving Timorese police officers. It also detracted from more serious problems, such as the terrible state of the roads, which is continuing to impede economic development and making travel in many directions beyond the capital downright treacherous.

UNMIT seemed in no mood to stand its ground and discuss the allegation, even though many of the problems in the slide had been hinted at in much more careful language in previous reports to the Security Council. Instead, the head of the UN in Timor apologised. The natural inclination of the UN, donors, and NGOs seems to be either to say nothing and take it, or to cave in altogether.

It's enough to drive anyone to drink, which is what I was doing one night in Castaways. It was a typical torpid night, with harried waitstaff serving glutinous chicken parmigiana to depressed government advisers. My companion was a forlorn Australian ex-public servant frustrated at his inability to get anywhere in his efforts to reform the Timorese civil service. He looked ready to throw himself off the balustrade. He had just finished an 11-month stint, and made what I now regard as the second of the two most profound statements I heard in my time in Dili. Sipping his lukewarm beer, he said, 'If Australia was serious about being effective, they wouldn't hire people like me — English-speaking civil servants, here for short stints, who cannot interact with their Timorese counterparts. They'd hire people on long-term contracts, and compel them to learn the language. I'm fed up and not coming back. I'm useless here.' Such self-awareness and honesty was refreshing, but not permanent. I bumped into the same gentleman about a year later, back on a 'short-term consulting assignment, in and out — you know how it goes', and found him as frustrated as ever. The Timorese still weren't listening, and the embassy still didn't want to know. I was reminded that it is the physicians who find it most difficult to heal themselves. Maybe it is the human condition, but it is something that bureaucrats too often eliminate from their reports.

However, simply firing broadsides against foreign-aid workers in Timor would be neither fair nor accurate. I met many dedicated people in the field, and what united many of them was that few fitted easily into the bureaucratic mould. In the eastern town of Lospalos, I met a family of American evangelical missionaries — the husband working as a carpenter, and his wife as a doctor in the local hospital. Their kids spoke the local Fataluku language fluently, and she had given birth to her son in the local hospital. Their comportment reminded me of the family in the beginning of the novel *The Poisonwood Bible*, only without the deranged father. The family radiated decency and clean living. On another occasion in the same town, I met another person who also seemed very decent — a Brazilian missionary who railed against the ineptitude of the police.

The legacy of another remarkable man is to be found not far from the rebel leader Gastao Salsinha's home in the hill-town of Gleno. Down a hollow in the road is a place called the Familia Hope orphanage, run for many years by an irrepressible great bear of an Australian called Isa Bradridge. He had come in 1999 because, he said, he had received something akin to a sacred calling. The compound is an attestation to what human decency can achieve. Relying often on little more than a sense of what was right, Isa carved out this home in the hills for over forty children who were either without parents or who had somehow been abandoned by their families. His residential institution was one of the neatest and best-kept places that I'd ever come across in the country. Like the NGO *La'o Hamutuk*, it is medicinal for the soul to visit there. By the time I got to know him, his work was done. The children had now grown into teenagers and young adults, and had taken over the running of the centre for him. He left for Australia in early 2012.

I passed by the orphanage one day with another singular expatriate, a New Zealander with tight, blonde curls called Keryn Clarke whose family are long-standing residents of Sydney. Our destination was the village of Fatubolu higher up the mountain, and we were on our way to a ceremony to mark the official opening of the hamlet's first water pump. Before the installation of the pump, the villagers (and often the women) had had to hike over a mountain to lug water to wash and cook with; the spigot offered the potential of making their lives a lot easier.

Keryn's road to Fatubolu had begun over fifteen years earlier in a city called Kuito in Angola, where she had been working as an aid worker. On the only remaining wall of a bombed-out building, someone had daubed the words 'Viva Xanana', thereby providing her first inkling of the country where she would spend the next decade and more. Arriving in the tinderbox city of Dili in 1998 to work for Oxfam Community Aid Abroad (her minder was my old boss, Francisco), she has been living in Timor more or less ever since — through the missed opportunities of UN administration, independence, and the internal crumbling of 2006, when the country turned on itself. She always strikes me as effortlessly endearing and sunny, but there is also a dogged and persevering quality to her. While working for Oxfam, she had helped to act at the helm of the advocacy campaign to shame the Australian government into giving Timor a fair share of the resources within the Timor Sea. Now, she fights through thickets of bureaucracy to help provide water to rural districts. The program's goal is to deliver water to nearly 10 per cent of the population who, despite the money sloshing around in Dili, have received only glancing benefits from it.

Keryn seems to be one of those people who knows everyone and is known by everyone. Not only is she integrated broadly within the community's field of work, but she seems to carry the sense that she's in it for the long haul and that it is natural there will be as many failures and missteps as there are successes.

Even by the immoderate standards of Timorese ceremonies, she was greeted with acclaim, and we were treated to a welcoming party even more elaborate than the one prepared for the local parliamentarian, who was also attending. A large crowd was gathered on the fringe of the village, with members of the various different layers of authority — chiefs of the village, chiefs of the hamlets, spiritual leaders — at the front of them all. Men were lustily blowing on cow horns and others sang incantations, their hands raised in the air in a gesture that I recognised as one used to summon the spirits. And this was only the beginning. Thereafter we were shepherded to a large tent in the centre of the village, where an MC with a bass-heavy sound system was whipping the assembled company into a frenzy with his hyperbole. The degree of excitement that a simple water pump was generating was illustrative of how little the people had. As is customary, the food had been prepared in advance of the ceremony, and plates of it sat to the side in the sweltering heat. A cake had also been prepared, which seemed to be in the process of being baked for a second time.

Clearly, this was the biggest thing to have taken place for many months, and the organisers squeezed every last drop out of it with prayers, a ritual chewing of the betel nut, and speeches — oh-so-many speeches, from practically everyone with a title in the hall who had had anything to do with the water pump. I wrote down eleven names in my notebook, and I'm not sure that was the final number. I wished I could have taken their unalloyed happiness home with me. The donor representative from the embassy thoroughly befuddled the gap-toothed audience with a long-winded explanation of how this project fitted into the Millennium Development Goals. The chief of police — I later found out he commanded the sum total of two men — used the opportunity to hand out a preposterous list of equipment demands to the visiting foreigners. A new car, he averred, was 'guaranteed' to provide security.

Keryn's name figured in almost all of the speeches. She and her team had spent years coming up to this village, which was about five hours' drive from Dili. They had negotiated all manner of problems regarding land, sitting down with the relevant authorities, and ensuring that everyone was consulted. The process of installing just one pump had spanned over two years. Many of the speakers recognised the duration of her stay in the country, and they hoped that she'd work to realise their next dream: a toilet. 'You need to be here a long time,' the police commander whispered to me as Keryn was getting her photo taken — no doubt wishing he'd typed up another funding letter to give to me. As we left, the party was only just getting started, with the electric synthesizer music of Timorese crooners being pumped out of the sound system. One of the old men who, earlier, had been blowing fervently on a cow horn, was beginning to dance to a hidden rhythm. 'We're going to dance until dawn,' he said. It was three o'clock in the afternoon.

There are many exceptional long-term expatriates like Keryn who live in Timor-Leste. Many became my good and true friends, and my only hesitation in trying to name them all is the danger of inadvertently leaving someone out. Some, like Keryn and, of even longer lineage, Charlie Scheiner, were drawn into Timor-Leste through their activism for the country's independence. Others have become involved through having met Timorese partners and then having moved there with them. Others probably fell into the country along the same trajectory that I did: they somehow came to work for a short time and found themselves extending their stay repeatedly. I knew mostly English-speaking long-stayers, but no doubt there are just as many among the Portuguese-speaking expatriates. Put together, they probably have achieved as much as all the phalanxes of workers combined who have stayed for short periods before heading off to other troubled lands in search of fortune and glory. The long-stay expatriates seem personally comfortable around Timorese, and have many contacts in their mobile-phone directories, which is essential for getting things accomplished in this land where all politics are personal.

All is most certainly not hopeless in terms of international assistance. To be effective, however, assistance work requires time, deep roots, and patience — qualities and attributes that are not always valued in donor organisations. The Tropical Bakery School of International Capacity-Building is of dubious value. Much longer apprenticeships are needed.

Chapter Ten

Far from Home

Dungannon and Portadown: Timorese speak of these small towns in the middle of Northern Ireland with something approaching reverence. 'What is Northern Ireland like?' asked Alfredo, my Tetun teacher of a few months. Ridiculously, I somehow thought he must have been inquiring about our peace process, so I tried to yammer out some explanation of our power-sharing agreement. He let me warble on for a while before he stopped me. 'Not that,' he said. 'The factories — I really want to go there.' I didn't have the first clue as to what he meant. As I searched for the equivalent English words in my dictionary, he slowly explained that many Timorese were now living close to where I was born. The vast majority were working in meat-processing plants, slicing up chickens, turkeys, and other dead animals and laying them out on plastic cartons for onward shipment to supermarket fridges and freezers. 'There are great opportunities there, and you can make lots and lots of money,' he declared. He painted my home as a land of plenty in just the same way that young Irish men and women dream about the United States and, increasingly, Australia. 'You come here to make money, and we go there,' he observed. 'The world is really strange.'

No matter where I was in Timor-Leste, mentioning that I came from Northern Ireland would provoke the same smiling reaction. Eyes would light up, and Timorese would tell me about friends or relatives who lived there and the lavish lifestyle that they were apparently leading. I was shown photo albums of sons and daughters posed smiling in shopping centres, dancing the *tebe tebe* dance at community halls, and lots of pictures of food. On Facebook, I read the green-eyed comments that friends in Dili made about pictures posted by young Timorese men in Ireland looking very pleased with themselves in cheesy nightclubs. Some knew comically little about the country where their family members were living. One picture showed a daughter arm-in-arm with a tall and well-built black man, who was her partner. 'Where is he from?' I asked. 'Northern Ireland,' was the reply. 'That is the colour of Irish people's skin.'

The wages earned half a world away were changing lives back home for the better. Many of the men of Atauro, the island just over the water from Dili that both the Portuguese and the Indonesians had used as a prison, were now in Northern Ireland. In this place, at least, one of the first uses of the money remitted back seemed to be the purchase of a large TV and a thumping stereo system that blared pop music long into the night. This meant that their houses could often be heard before they could be seen. 'I really want to go to that magical island, Ireland,' said a Timorese to me as we walked past a house that belonged to a man living, apparently, in Dungannon. At that point, I just wanted to get far away from the din.

In some ways, Timor-Leste very much reminds me of my own island home. The fact that Timorese will prejudge an individual on knowledge of another family member, or on the basis of where they come from, seems entirely normal to me: it's what happens in all small, cramped places where it is hard to escape from the past. Intensely personal politics is another Irish normality, where one's family name and personal history is every bit as important as institutional titles and positions.

The two faraway countries also share certain political and historical resemblances. Both have had long colonial occupations, both are divided islands, and, pertaining to the Republic of Ireland, both have two official languages, only one of which is commonly spoken. Catholicism is the common, dominant religion, on both islands.

The linkage is not just one of comparative history. Although the new immigrants come to Northern Ireland, a part of the United Kingdom, the origins of the close bond lie over the border in the Republic of Ireland and have to do with a remarkable man called Tom Hyland. Tom was a then-unemployed bus driver who cheerfully admits to having never heard of Timor-Leste until he happened to be watching TV one evening in 1992 in his flat in inner-city Dublin. What he saw would change his life forever. The programme he watched was called *Death of a Nation*, and it contained undercover footage of the carnage at Santa Cruz cemetery in Dili on the day that Indonesian troops fired into a crowd of demonstrators. More than 250 Timorese were killed that day, their bodies carted off and dumped in unmarked graves or flung into the sea. 'Shocking', said his companion, turning off the TV and getting ready for bed. But something about the programme fired Tom into action. Almost single-handedly, he began mobilising to cajole and embarrass the Irish government into not only changing its policy towards the Indonesian occupation but also advocating for Timor-Leste within the community of nations. He cajoled the Dublin City Council to name a public park 'East Timor Park' in solidarity with the Timorese people, and coordinated a candlelit vigil outside a state dinner for a visiting Australian prime minister in order to draw attention to Australia's culpability during the Indonesian occupation. The Irish foreign minister was persuaded to crouch inside a makeshift cell on a busy Dublin street. The foreign minister wore a headband that said simply 'Free Xanana', and the scene succeeded in doing what Tom intended — it drew attention to the plight of Timorese leaders in Indonesian jails. The pictures made headline news. During this time, his house became a magnet for Timorese to visit and to plan agitation from; Jose Belo, the journalist, came to visit in 1996.

Tom's ceaseless efforts to embarrass those in the corridors of power are well recognised. Now, living in Dili, where he teaches English to Timorese diplomats, he has received one of the country's highest honours after independence. What I find most remarkable, however, is that he seems to be known by everyone, from politicians to kids on the street. One of his former students told me that even those children born after 1999 know who Tom Hyland is, because of his remarkable contribution and his willingness to continue helping the country by teaching English. He is further evidence of how spending time pays dividends in this land of connections.

He is also Ireland's honorary consul to Timor-Leste, and Timor-Leste's honorary consul to Ireland — raising the possibility of him being able to call a meeting with himself. His doggedness contributed to Ireland setting up a mission in Dili, its farthest-flung outpost. (My wife and I celebrated our wedding party there in 2010.) Since then, Ireland's mission has closed its doors. Despite Ireland having spent nearly US$50 million in aid to Timor-Leste over the last ten years, the remittances sent back to Northern Ireland were perhaps the most tangible product. Tom is one of those relatively unlikely Irish people who have become quite well known because of Ireland's elevated profile, which he himself did so much to engineer.

I was often asked whether I knew a woman called Bernadette McAliskey. The frail, whiskery man who first mentioned her name lived in a small village, way in the east of the country that was two hours down a bone-shuddering road, and his question was so incongruous that I had to ask him to repeat it three times just so I heard him right. Her name is as well known to my generation as the name Xanana would be to Timorese, but it isn't one that I would have thought would have carried all the way to rural villages more than half a world away. Bernadette Devlin, as she was then known — a feisty nationalist politician who campaigned for the rights of her community in Northern Ireland — was the youngest-ever person elected to the House of Commons. I remember reading that, much later, she'd broken with leading Irish republican leaders such as Gerry Adams and Martin McGuiness, who signed up to a peace agreement with the British government and the Protestant Unionist political parties, but I'd lost track of her career since then. The old man did not know her for those reasons, but because she was now involved in helping Timorese settle into their new homes in Northern Ireland. 'I'm too old,' he said, 'but if I was a young man I'd want to go to Ireland, too.' A large number of the men in his village had left already. You could tell which ones just by looking around; their families' homes were bigger and better built than the rest.

How the Timorese ended up in Dungannon and Portadown is a classic story of chain migration. The story goes that a Northern Irish recruitment agency went to northern Portugal in the late 1990s with the aim of hiring some of the local men, who were apparently famed for their butchering skills. One Timorese man from the small community who lived in Portugal happened to be at the job fair, and he signed up to go to Northern Ireland. He was followed by one friend and then another, each sending back word of plentiful jobs. Through a loophole kept open during the Indonesian occupation and never subsequently closed, Timorese are eligible for Portuguese citizenship, which duly entitles them to work in all the countries of the European Union. No one knows the true figures, but there are estimated to be several thousand Timorese in Northern Ireland, and even more in England — mostly in Manchester, Oxford, and Peterborough. (Very few are in the Republic of Ireland.) More and more of their friends and family are anxious to follow them. Each weekday morning, hundreds of Timorese wait outside the Portuguese embassy in Dili, clutching birth certificates and other documentation needed to secure the precious red passport. Men with families leave their wives and children for years on end to go to Northern Ireland, while many young men are foregoing opportunities to pursue higher education in Timor-Leste or Indonesia to strike out for their El Dorado. This new group of emigrants aren't members of the elite or the Dili business set, but are drawn from the rural poor. Many, I would learn, had not even completed a high-school education, and Dili was the farthest place they had ever previously travelled to.

I didn't really know what to make of all this adoration of Northern Ireland. Few of my family and friends could reliably have located Timor-Leste on a map, but there was much awareness of the island of Ireland and one part in particular in this little corner in Asia. I was born and grew up in a town about sixty miles away from Dungannon and Portadown, and while I didn't know these towns well at all, I found it hard to conceive of them as centres of plenty. These areas in the west of the province are traditionally thought of as being among the most deprived of places, not just in Northern Ireland but in the entire United Kingdom. I remember passing through Dungannon as a child, and I thought it as bleak and damp as many other towns on our journey. Portadown was an old industrial town synonymous with disputes over Orange marches. It was associated with a sectarianism even more bitter and entrenched than elsewhere in Northern Ireland, which was no mean feat. As a child, we'd heard bogeymen stories about a Protestant paramilitary leader called King Rat who operated out of the Brownstown estate on the edge of the town. I'd been to Portadown once, too, and hadn't really envisaged the need to return. Friends from there had moved away to the United States in search of work and opportunity, and many didn't relish the prospect of returning. 'It's a fucking dump,' I remember one of them saying. 'I'll never be back.' I was intrigued by how highly the Timorese talked up these places in a way that might even have surprised their residents. On a trip home, I decided to see if the streets of mid-Ulster were truly paved with gold.

My first stop was Dungannon, where I found my childhood memories to be sadly accurate. The weather was overcast, and the town every bit as bleak and gloomy as I remembered it. El Dorado it most certainly was not; the closest thing I would see to a city of gold was the name of one of the slot machines on which a Timorese youth was playing in a poorly lit 'amusement centre'. The storefronts in the town centre included a cheque-cashing store, a betting shop, an employment agency, or a place to buy second-hand clothes. But something about the town was definitely different. Hundreds of Timorese, mostly men, wandered the streets, many dressed in cheap-looking shell-suits that must have been wholly inadequate to shield them from the damp, grey cold. They seemed to keep to themselves, bundled in their hats, with their heads down. The scene was beyond being out of place — I was so astonished that I nearly ended up driving into the first Timorese I saw. Just as surprising was the sight of official signs written in Tetun. Not least, outside a large fortified building on the way into town was written the words *Benvindo mai eskuadra Polisia Dungannon* ('Welcome to the Dungannon police station').

Timorese are not the only new arrivals into Dungannon. Also working there, mostly in the factories, are labourers drawn from Brazil, Portugal and its former colonies in Africa, and many countries in Eastern Europe. This small market-town of about 20,000 people is among the most ethnically diverse in all of Northern Ireland, and the immigrant community is large enough to support an ethnic food store catering to various tastes, run by a small, spry, bearded man from India who wore a greatcoat and stamped his feet repeatedly in a probably hopeless effort to keep warm. The culinary enclave reminded me of the shops on the east coast of the United States where wistful young Irish carpenters and labourers can stock up on black pudding and potato bread. With an eye to the Timorese clientele, there was a shop selling spinach and chillies (which can be pounded into the fiery *ai-manas* sauce that is as ubiquitous an accompaniment to a Timorese meal as tomato ketchup would be to Irish fare). The town was multicultural, but it hardly struck me as a melting pot. The local people and the new immigrants passed each other on the pavements as if shielded from one another.

Across from the ethnic food shop was a branch of the Ulster bank. It was there that I met Justin, who was queuing up to use the ATM. He nearly choked on his cigarette when I started speaking in Tetun to him. 'I simply don't believe this,' he said. 'Who was the witch that put a spell on you?' His original intention had been to head down to the bookmaker to place a few bets — a way of whiling away his day off — but, instead, he invited me home to meet his friends. 'They'll not believe me if I tell them,' he said, still somewhat flabbergasted. We walked down towards the house, and on the way met one of his roommates, his cousin, who, enticed by the stories of free and easy money in Northern Ireland, had arrived six months before. As yet, he had not been able to find any work.

The factories were full to capacity, and the cousin spent his days wandering around town trying to keep warm. Before arriving, he said that only on TV had he ever seen anyone wearing a coat.

Their brown, pebble-dash house was opposite a patch of rough ground, and from the outside it looked like it had seen much better days. Probably built before home insulation, the house felt even chillier inside than out, and smelled slightly of an unpleasant musk that might well have been the latter stages of rising damp. There was no heating at all, save for an electric fire in the living room that emitted a dry, shimmery warmth which vanished as soon the fire was turned off. The flimsy curtains reminded me of stylised shows about the 1970s.

A grand total of eleven men lived in the three-bedroomed house; they slept in shifts on the beds. All came from the sub-district of Baguia in the east of Timor-Leste. Six of them were working, and five were still looking for work — no doubt a burden to those in employment. They were paid the equivalent of about US$10 an hour, with a little extra for overtime. It was a relative fortune by Timorese standards; but, once they subtracted the money sent back, tax, rent, and the exorbitant fee to wire money back to Timor (as much as 18 per cent of the amount being transferred), there was not a lot of money to spare.

They all seemed like nice guys, and I ended up spending the day with them. We dispatched one fellow to the corner shop to get some beer; then, having recently been in Dili, I was able to fill them in on all the latest political shenanigans and intrigues. Surmising, rightly, that that this would go down well, I'd brought some copies of *Tempo Semanal* with me, and they shook their heads at the stories of shifty business-dealings back in their home country.

My unexpected arrival seemed like a welcome respite from their usual monotonous routine of staring at a TV screen that transmitted programs in a language they couldn't understand. They relished the opportunity to pepper me with questions about Northern Ireland that they'd wanted to know the answers to for years. What was the problem between Catholics and Protestants? Was it resolved? Who or what was Sinn Fein? Why did emotions rise among local people on 12 July, the anniversary of the battle won by a Protestant king over his Catholic foe in 1690? What was Gaelic football? Why do people drink so much all the time? From what they said, this was even more of an alien land to them than Timor-Leste had been to me when I had first arrived. Buying a mobile-phone contract or bus tickets, cleaning a toilet, or ordering food off a menu — all this befuddled them, as did the concept of a functioning postal service. I was the first Irish person whom they had ever had a meaningful conversation with. It seemed that their only social interaction with a local had been with their landlady, when she appeared once a month to collect the rent.

We had a tasty lunch of chicken, rice, spinach, and *ai-manas* sauce that tasted identical to something they might have eaten in Timor-Leste, with one important difference: here in Northen Ireland, they had no women to prepare it. As well as having to do the cleaning, they had all had to learn how to cook. I asked them what they thought of Western food, and they wrinkled their noses. Most had tried hamburgers and pizzas, but hadn't taken to them. In terms of the degree of integration into my country, they seemed as connected as the average denizen of Castaways was in theirs. The major difference, I suppose, was that while Justin was paid just slightly above the minimum wage to pluck chickens in Dungannon, the Castaways wolfing down chicken burgers in Dili bars were paid hundreds of times more to deliver a far less tangible product.

'Some things about this country are amazing, though,' said Domingos, the smallest and most wiry of all the men who puffed hungrily on one of the pungent clove cigarettes I'd brought from Dili, flicking the ash into the empty fireplace. 'The roads are good, the hospitals are clean, and what's amazing is that the people get paid even if they don't work — something called "Job Centre" ...' he said, using the only two words in English that he seemed to know. His friends nodded in agreement. It was interesting to hear how they viewed my country, a place slowly recovering from its own troubled past and which, to me, still has many remnants of bitterness, division, and cronyism in its politics. Now it was my turn to look surprised and pleased. But their experiences of racism and small-town prejudice made me ashamed and sad. A nation of immigrants wasn't being universally welcoming to many of their new visitors who were, like so many immigrants around the world, doing jobs that the locals felt it beneath themselves to do. At some point, all the guys had been the victims of racist taunts on the street, such as 'Brown monkey' and 'Go back to Africa'. Bricks had been thrown at their houses, and they knew of some Timorese in other areas who'd fled their homes following sectarian violence. I thought of the local man who served me breakfast at my hotel, who had cheerily told me, 'We don't like them — they're foreigners, you know.' He must have pegged me as someone in whom it would be safe to confide his prejudiced confidences.

My hosts' home area of Baguia was a hotbed of Timorese resistance activity, and the home area of Taur Matan Ruak, the prominent army commander and now the president. As young boys, some of the men had played important bit-part roles in sustaining the resistance fighters, delivering notes and supplies in the dead of night. They told me they would sneak out from their homes under cover of darkness, trek for hours up the mountain tracks, and then scramble back before dawn so that any Timorese in the pay of the Indonesians wouldn't notice their absence. They enjoyed talking about the resistance time, as it seemed to bring them back to their mountain homes where, all things being equal, they probably wanted to be.

The men were clearly lonely here, shivering by the electric heater, linguistically cut off from everyone around them, and nostalgically longing for home. I asked them why they didn't want to go back. In part, I rightly assumed it was a matter of pride; they'd been sending glowing reports back home, and would be embarrassed to 'fess up that the reality wasn't anywhere near as rosy. Another reason was financial: people back home were relying on their money. Now that I think about it, perhaps this aspect of their situation is another parallel with that of the 'expert' advisers in Timor-Leste.

But another part of them seemed to think that getting a guaranteed wage in a chicken factory in a cold country that was forever shrouded in grey cloud was still superior to returning both to the entangled politics of family and history in Timor-Leste and to limited opportunities. The money they earned was theirs to do with as they wanted. And it was paid on time, as per the terms of their contract — a matter-of-fact reality they found astonishing. Despite all the new money in Timor-Leste and their leaders' talk of a bright new tomorrow, they considered that living in a near-permanent state of disorientation in Northern Ireland was a more sensible proposition than trying to make it at home. 'In Timor-Leste you need to know someone to get the state's money, and we're not from the right families,' said one man, uttering a hangdog lament I had heard often during my years in Dili. It seemed that independence had lost some of its lustre for the working man: back in Baguia, the roads were still atrocious; and if the migrant workers returned, they'd be scraping out a subsistence life on the land. It wasn't delivered as such, but it was a devastating indictment on their Timorese homeland, and perhaps an acknowledgement that the original expectations of what would follow independence were unrealistic.

All told, I spent about a week shuttling between the towns of mid-Ulster, either meeting Timorese relatives of friends in Dili or randomly ingratiating myself by speaking in impromptu Tetun to people I met on the street. As with all immigrant communities, their experiences were mixed. Some of the Timorese, particularly those who had learned some English, seemed to be faring reasonably well, and had even picked up on some of the alcohol-based subtleties of Irish culture, like buying a round of drinks. I spent a happy afternoon before Christmas knocking back pints of Guinness in a pub in Dungannon with a group of young men from Dili who were able to josh comfortably in English and spoke in Irish accents so strong that it sounded as though they'd been born there. My son was about six months at the time, and he giggled with delight as he was passed from person to person. Even in the heat of the pub, the guys did not take off either their beanies or their jackets; they said that the sense of feeling cold never left them.

I even bumped into some of the ex-petitioners who had mutinied against the army in 2006; they had used the payment from the government to buy a ticket and head over to Northern Ireland, too. I met them in the closest approximation to El Dorado I would find there; they were sliding tokens into a poker machine with circa-1995 graphics. The men revelled in their relative infamy, but were clearly disappointed that no one in Northern Ireland had heard of the petitioners. 'I was on CNN once,' one of them sighed ruefully. The slots in the poker machines had Tetun instructions on them, revealing just how many of the clientele were Timorese, and enabling equal-opportunity exploitation.

Others seemed unsettled and melancholic, and probably had symptoms of depression. In Portadown, I'd been asked to check on a young Timorese fellow from the same area in Viqueque where Abilio and Jose lived. As it turned out, he lived on the Brownstown estate, the former home of King Rat. The contrast between his steamy jungle home and the coffee shop where we went could not have been starker. It was just before Christmas, and the town centre's bustle only made him feel more disoriented. 'I feel so alone here,' he said, his lip quivering over his cup. Yes, he was earning a comparative fortune in comparison to what he would earn in Timor-Leste, but this was an expensive country, and it was difficult to live well here and send money back home. The no doubt under-the-counter cigarettes with Cyrillic writing that he was smoking were the cheapest he could buy; even then, they were seven times the price of a pack back home. On my return, his family asked me how he was, and I hedged my reply. I told them he seemed sad about being away for Christmas, but otherwise was well. I, too, was gilding the truth; there seemed an awful lot of this positive spinning going on.

It wasn't just the ex-petitioners who were spending a lot of time and money gambling. I saw many Timorese who seemed to be frittering much of their money away. One bookmaker's shop was just up from the hotel in Dungannon where I stayed, and a steady stream of Timorese were constantly coming in and out of its doors. The clerk told me that they were his best customers — although he thought, probably accurately, that many were spending their time in the bookies to ward off the cold. 'Where is East Timor, actually?' the man asked. He thought it was somewhere near South Africa. The overwhelming sense I took away with me was one of their loneliness and dislocation. Paradoxically, separation from their extended families and the men's acute sense of them being very far away was only heightened by the exchange of text messages, telephone calls, and Skype conversations.

'I can understand why Timorese don't report the racism incidents,' said Bernadette McAliskey when I went around to meet her. 'But that doesn't make it any more acceptable.' I'd always wanted to meet Bernadette, but could never have imagined that it would have been in the context of talking about immigrants from a faraway land. She runs a sort of souped-up social-welfare clinic and walk-in welfare advice centre for Timorese and other immigrants, based in a dingy business park on the outskirts of Dungannon. Her centre is called the South Tyrone Empowerment Program, and offers advice on welfare benefits as well as teaching life skills and providing an array of training courses, including English lessons. It was a busy place. The waiting room was full when I arrived, and the whole office hummed with a grim-faced earnestness and sense of purpose I've rarely seen in any place of work. The contrast between it and the fairly esoteric initiatives on conflict resolution and peace building that the Irish government had lavished money on back in Timor-Leste could not have been any greater. This was unglamorous and never-ending slog work, with small and occasional victories against bureaucracy as the only consolation. It was a world away from the gilded domains that her former political travellers in the power-sharing administration now inhabited. The chunky mobile phone on her desk looked as if it was one of the first products ever to have rolled off the Nokia production line.

Bernadette looked totally worn out. It was the last working afternoon before the Christmas holidays, and she was understandably preoccupied with tasks that needed to be finished. But the topic seemed to reanimate her, and I soon realised that this was the same feisty, opinionated, and eloquent woman who had stood up for the rights of Catholic nationalists in Northern Ireland, from a time before I was born. She credited the factory owners for being fair employers, but rattled off the everyday problems that Timorese faced in accessing the health, welfare, and local government systems — problems compounded both by the language gap, but also by a reluctance on the part of people in Dungannon to fully accept the Timorese in their midst. 'You're a foreigner here,' she said. 'You'd understand.' And, although this was said slightly for dramatic effect, she was right. The elastic-band ball of interfamilial connections and family names in Dungannon was very different from that in the part of Northern Ireland that I came from. This was a place where friendships were made at school and where they endured. I could imagine that I would have had a hard time fully integrating myself into this place. I knew of friends from England and Canada who had lived in Northern Ireland, and who found that, no matter what they did, they could never fit in. I could easily imagine how difficult it would be for someone from half a world away. 'These people are at the bottom rung in this society,' she said. The fact that the Timorese seemed so grateful with their position, despite being jammed into the kind of cold, damp houses that Justin and his friends lived in, amid all their family privations, made her wonder just how tough the life was that they'd left behind.

Her sense was that the Timorese community in Dungannon was there to stay. Increasingly, women were coming over to join their husbands, and Timorese children were being born there. For many, it was no longer a place to go to just to make some money before returning home. A little piece of Timor-Leste was being carved out in my home country, its very existence a reflection of the challenges back in their homeland.

I asked Bernadette about the Timorese officials and politicians who'd called into Dungannon over the years, and she rolled her eyes. Visiting consuls, ambassadors, and ministers had made many promises to the Timorese to improve their lot. Her organisation had been involved in facilitating many of those visits, but she had heard of little follow-up after the dignitaries had left, leaving it for her little NGO to fill the gaps.

Their promises were as bombastic, sincere at the time, and ultimately ephemeral as those tendered by foreign dignitaries who visited Timor-Leste. Some of their bluster must have worn off, including a taste for living well. I told her a story I'd heard about a senior official flown at great expense to Belfast to attend a workshop on gender. The individual in question was reputed to have refused to leave her hotel room until the exorbitant daily allowance was pushed through the door. 'Many of the Timorese politicians struck me as being as craven, pompous, and self-interested as our own are nowadays,' said Bernadette, with a sigh. It was a winning line, and I wrote it down and asked her if I could use it in this book. She thought for a second. 'You absolutely can,' she said, as a big, impish smile broke across her face.

Epilogue

The Hotel Timor was unnaturally quiet at mid-morning on the day of the presidential election. In the absence of several dozen clove-tobacco cigarettes, the air quality was no doubt at unprecedentedly high levels. This was because there was no one there. There were no spivs, businessmen, or any of their hangers-on to be seen. Even the Portuguese police officers, who usually lingered long over their espressos in a manner probably reminiscent of their predecessors in the years and centuries before, were absent. The only other person in the coffee shop with me was Jose Belo, the journalist, who was single-handedly trying to re-smoke the premises.

I'd arrived back in Dili that morning on the early-morning flight from Darwin. Waiting in the check-in queue, I started talking to an Australian who had been working for the previous six months as a 'capacity builder' in the Ministry of Agriculture. 'Mariano must be very busy these days with the parliamentary election coming up,' I said, referring to the minister — a former student activist, an up-and-comer in the small political elite, and the reputed owner of a new Hummer. 'Who's that?' asked the Australian. The minister had been in the newspapers practically every day of late, 'guaranteeing' something or other, but it seemed that blanket coverage was not enough to get him noticed. At the duty-free, I saw a middle-aged

East Timorese man buy a $200 bottle of whisky. He paid for the liquor with two crisp notes drawn out of a thick-set white envelope.

After checking in to my hotel, I wandered around a few polling stations to see what was going on. It was all quiet at each place, with the Timorese police sitting under trees, or perched on the porches of a building close by, for respite from the sun's glare. Along the way, I bumped into Charlie Scheiner, who was pleased to report that the poll was proceeding quietly in each of the stations in the capital that he'd visited. 'I've told journalists covering the election that Timor-Leste is becoming a normal country,' he said. There was little headline news here anymore, and the longer-term structural challenges that the country faced were, he said, not of as much interest to foreign media. He rattled off a series of grim statistics and development indicators. I admired Charlie's indefatigability and deep-set affection for this place. He was truly in it for the long haul.

Jose was contemplating what he was confident was a job well done. In the previous few months he had taken a sabbatical from pestering politicians at *Tempo Semanal* in order to work for a man who wanted to become one. Since the beginning of the year, he had steered the campaign of Taur Matan Ruak, the former chief of the army who was bidding to become head of state. An observer who was usually cynical now sounded smitten. Taur, he said, was a man different from all the rest. He had clean hands, a clear mind, and the nation's best interests at heart. Jose had been one of Matan Ruak's most trusted messengers during the resistance, and had been a leading figure in 'Team Success', the peculiar English-language designation that everyone seemed to use for his campaign team.

The ex-general's campaign was a case study in the shifting sands and downright peculiarity of Timorese politics. One would expect the strong backing he received from resistance fighters and activists-turned-businessmen, but his campaign also harnessed some of the renegade petitioners who had mutinied against Matan Ruak when he'd been head of the army in 2006. Six years later, on a stage in Dili, many of the formerly rebellious soldiers swayed arm-in-arm with the candidate, to cheesy pop music. This was after, one by one, each man had burst onto the stage, their pumped-up style reminiscent of football players before the Super Bowl. I knew all this because I had watched the video on YouTube, the crowd going nuts as the MC cheered each name, announcing his arrival. It didn't really make sense how quickly enemies had become friends. Rai Los, the former head of the shady militia in 2006, given arms by Rogerio Lobato, and now a leading businessman and regular denizen of the Hotel Timor, was supporting Matan Ruak, too. Like many of the political alliances in Timor-Leste, this rainbow coalition defied rational analysis. It was a confusion of loyalties, but it seemed to work.

'So, do you want to meet Taur?' said Jose. He knew what the answer was, and he was on his mobile phone to arrange the meeting before I could even reply. I paid up and hopped in his car, and we drove out in the direction of the beachfront on the east side of town, veering sharply off the road at one point and up an unpaved hilly track where, perched at the top, was a half-built house. It was Matan Ruak's brother's home, and he was using it as the place where he conducted media interviews. When he arrived, the candidate had just returned from casting his ballot. His right index finger was stained with the indelible dye given to all voters to prevent anyone from engaging in any double-voting. He was a slender man who looked very different from the rangy, long-haired military leader of the resistance. Unlike many of his other colleagues who had filled out considerably since becoming part of the post-independence elite, he was still rake-thin. Tinted spectacles now protected his sharp eyes, which were apparently badly deteriorated from his having spent too many years outside, squinting in the sun.

He directed Jose and me to a table inside the unfinished part of the house, a section protected from the elements by a wispy, blue tarpaulin. We were joined by another of his campaign staff, a middle-aged Portuguese woman, Paula Pinto, who had a remarkable capacity for chain-smoking cigarettes. Her own connection with Timor went back many years. Her husband was Roque Rodrigues — one of the revolutionaries of 1975, who, upon returning to Timor, had become both Matan Ruak's civilian boss as secretary of defence and his housemate. He once said something to me that stuck in my mind. 'Sr Gordon, you must understand that in this country the past is important. No conceptual framework of anthropology is enough to explain Timor-Leste, so how can a simple policy? It cannot.'

The unfinished house was an appealing metaphor for the country that Taur Matan Ruak inherited a month later. Although Timor-Leste had come a long way in the previous ten years, realising the dream of independence was still very much a half-completed project. He rattled off a litany of woes besetting his compatriots: grinding rural poverty and isolation, frustrated and unfulfilled youth, appalling road infrastructure, poor governance, an unproductive services sector, unequal treatment of women, and signs of conspicuous consumption that was hard to tally with relatively low wages. It sounded like the sort of list that donors in Dili would say behind closed doors, but would never publicly utter for fear of speaking truth to power. 'Fighting a war was easy,' he said. 'To give food to people, to give work to people, to provide homes for people, to give clean water to people, to make a good life for people, that is the difficult part.' He referenced another former Portuguese colony, Guinea-Bissau, as an exemplar of the type of state and government he did not want Timor-Leste to become. At no point during the conversation did he make a single mention of international donors or the United Nations. This was a Timorese responsibility now. There could be no one to blame anymore but themselves.

He was optimistic that he could make a positive difference in people's lives. 'They said we would never get independence. We fought for it and we won it. Now, we must fulfil our dreams of what we want our freedom to be,' he said. 'We must work hard.' Over and over again during the speech at his inauguration ceremony a month later, he repeated the same refrain: 'We must work hard, we must work hard.' Good to his word, one of his first edicts as president was to insist that everyone be at their desks by eight in the morning, take no more than the stipulated lunch hour, and not leave any earlier than five o'clock.

But that was the future. On the way out, one of the bodyguards stopped to greet me. Everyone was baffled as to how we knew each other. I explained that I hadn't recognised him on the way in, but that he had placed me from the weeks I'd spent huffing and puffing in the humid Timorese police gym, trying to lose weight before I got married. 'Connections are important here,' I said, and the president-to-be nodded, as if someone, finally, had discovered this most obvious of truths.

The list is long of liberation movements that have fought lengthy wars in order to become independent, only to disappoint the aspirations of their people. Equally ignoble is the list of countries that have squandered their resource wealth. I really hope that this remarkable little country that has fought against all the odds to be recognised as a member of the community of nations doesn't squander the opportunity it now has. Light-headed on the money flowing in from resource revenues, some Timorese leaders are vaingloriously positioning their country as the next China, but the most urgent problems that need to be addressed are much closer to home, and require tough work rather than rhetorical flourishes. To invert the rhetorical structure of the poster in one of the government offices, it will require many to 'arrive early and leave late'. It will require hard work. The combination of a limited human-resource base, a high birth-rate, and the fact that the national language is spoken only on this half-island and nowhere else means that the odds are stacked against Timor-Leste. But the Timorese have shown before that they are adept at bucking the odds. Few would have given them a chance at shaking off the Indonesian occupation. Now they face an even bigger challenge — building a state of their own. Let us wish them well.

Acknowledgements

A friend visiting from Israel is mentioned fleetingly in the first pages of this book, but this brief mention doesn't do justice to his contribution. His name is Yoav Alon, and, if he hadn't encouraged me to believe that I had a book in me, I probably would never have embarked upon this whole crazy venture. Yoav convinced me that I should write a book about this mysterious and intriguing country, one that has never ceased to fascinate me. During a week-long road trip in Timor-Leste, we conceived the idea of a mix of history, memoir, and reportage.

The seed sown, many other people have given me great support in helping bring the book to fruition. A magnificent seven friends deserve thanks for going through both the initial treatment and, a year later, the entire manuscript. I can't thank enough Eddy Niesten, Matt Getz, Chris Patil, Rod Nixon, Cillian Nolan, David Roberts, and my brother, Patrick Peake. Their confidence in me spurred me on. Sue Halden-Brown was an excellent reader and writing coach, and Susan Cutsforth did a terrific job copy-editing the text.

For either reading the proposal, specific chapters, or both, I'd like to thank (in alphabetical order), Jenny Asman, Patrick Barron, Markus Bouillon, Edie Bowles, John Braithwaite, Kerry Brogan, Edyth Bulbring, Wayne Chambliss, James Cockayne, Jim Della-

Giacoma, Sinclair Dinnen, Dominick Donald, Richard Eves, Ceu Federer, Shepard Forman, Anthony Goldstone, Paul Hainsworth, Zoe Hawkins, Susan Heyward, Reyko Huang, Piers Kelly, John Lal, Sonja Litz, Piers Kelly, Lia Kent, Clara Lee, Francesco Mancini, Otwin Marenin, Flavio Simoes Martins, Patrick McAlinden, Stephen McCloskey, Martin McKee, Andrew McWilliam, Pia Oberoi, Lorna Fox O'Mahony, Marie Phillips, Mike Pugh, Janine Rauch, Elizabeth Reid, Anacleto da Costa Ribeiro, Kevin Rosser, Cyrus Samii, James Scambary, Charlie Scheiner, Graeme Smith, Jonny Steinberg, Kerry Taylor-Leech, Bu Wilson, and Michela Wrong.

Edward Rees was the person who convinced me all those years ago to go to Dili in the first place, and has been a strong supporter throughout the project. Michael J. Casey generously shared his proposal for his two books, which proved to be really useful as I was formulating my pitch. Renata Dwan told me not to write a sour-faced book, and I hope I've followed her advice. Julia Martin came up with the book's final title. Sam Roggeveen at *The Lowy Interpreter* gave me a platform to write some early pieces, and the feedback I received helped convince me to start writing the book.

Many of my Timorese friends were patient teachers. I'd like to extend my profound thanks to Jose Antonio Belo, Nelson Belo, and Joao Almeida Fernandes for their help and friendship throughout this project. Big thanks also must go (in alphabetical order) to Caetano Alves, Augusto Soares Baretto, Umbelina Belo, Maria Bernadino, Matias Boavida, Agustinho Caet, Aziu Coral, Damiao Correira, Faustino da Costa, Henrique da Costa, Alfredo Francisco, Alfredo Gama, Francisco da Costa Guterres, Frei Guterres, Veneranda Lemos, Moises Vicente Lopes, Fidelis Magalhaes, Lequi Mata, Julio Tomas Pinto, Roque Rodrigues, Antonio Campos Santos, Aderito Soares, Angela Tilman, Antonio

Viegas, and Manuel Viegas. I learned a great deal from working on a book of idioms with Anacleto da Costa Ribeiro, and I hope we publish this book some day.

Egidio Siga and Nelson de Mendonca were terrific research assistants as we explored together the world of the petitioner movement. Tom Hyland and Sophia Cason provided encouragement and telephone numbers throughout. Rob Wesley-Smith helped connect me with Niki Mutin. In West Timor, I'd like to thank Linda Boboy, my interpreter, and Anato Moreira, fix-it man *par excellence*. In Dungannon, I'd like to thank Bernadette and Roisin McAliskey, and the staff of the South Tyrone Empowerment Program.

Jill Jolliffe has been a dogged excavator of Timor-Leste's secrets for many years. She introduced me to my literary agent, John Timlin, who helped get the manuscript into the hands of publishers. I can't thank John enough for his bolshie persistence, good humour, and canny know-how. Henry Rosenbloom and his team at Scribe took a punt on an unknown writer, and I hope I've repaid their faith in me. Henry is a fearsomely good editor.

In Dili, I had two terrific bosses in Grant Edwards and Charmaine Quade, and I'd like to thank all my former colleagues from the Timor-Leste Police Development Program for being so tolerant of the Irishman in their midst. Ray Murray deserves a special mention for being such a terrific colleague and friend. In Canberra, the State, Society and Governance in Melanesia Program at the Australian National University provided me with an office to write the book.

I have a wonderful family. Both my mother and father have been incredibly generous and supportive to me, in good times and bad, and I hope I can be at least half as good a parent to my children as they have been to me. My siblings Mary, William, Nigel and Patrick, and my brother-in-law, Conor Rice, have all been very supportive. I've talked about the book so much to my godson, Conan Hinds, that I'm sure he will write a 'Horrible Histories' of Timor-Leste one day.

My wife, Suzanne McCourt, is my best friend and my biggest supporter. When I came up with the idea of a book, she was more than seven months pregnant, and took the idea of me embarking on an uncertain career as a writer with preternatural good cheer. She has much more faith in me than I often have in myself, and I love her more than words can say. And, as for our son Charlie, who has been around from Chapter Two onwards, well, let's just say I'd need another book to describe what a wonderful little guy he is and how happy he makes me. When's he older, I hope this book will help him understand Timor-Leste — the place that gave him his very existence and his second name, and which fascinates his father so.

A luta continua.

Abbreviations

CAVR: The Commission for Reception, Truth and Reconciliation in Timor-Leste

CNRT: The National Council of Timorese Resistance

FALINTIL: The Armed Forces for the National Liberation of Timor-Leste

F-FDTL: FALINTIL Defence Forces of Timor-Leste

FRETILIN: The Revolutionary Front for an Independent Timor-Leste

MAHIDI: pro-Indonesian militia acronym: 'Dead or Alive, for Integration with Indonesia'

NGO: Non-Government Organisation

UNDP: United Nations Development Program

UNMIT: United Nations Integrated Mission in Timor-Leste

UNPOL: United Nations Police

Sources and Further Reading

This book is based on a combination of interviews, conversations, travels, and recollections, some of which are drawn from my time living in Dili from 2007 to 2011. The interviews with characters such as Rogerio Lobato and Gastao Salsinha and travels through West Timor and Northern Ireland took place during the latter part of 2011 and the early half of 2012.

As would be clear from reading the text, Timor-Leste is a place where there is no consensus on what is objective 'truth'. Facts are not clear-cut and unambiguous in this land of rumours and intrigue. I have attempted to confirm the veracity of all the stories that I tell throughout this book. Any mistakes in the text are, of course, my own.

Written sources I have used include books, scholarly articles, pieces by NGOs, blogs, and email correspondence. I have mentioned many of the sources in the text, but I have grouped some of the source material thematically below, in the hope that readers interested in specific issues may find this a useful resource for further reading. The best means for readers to keep up to date with developments in Timor-Leste is to subscribe to the news service of the East Timor and Indonesia Action Network (ETAN). This is a tremendous resource, run on a shoestring by the indomitable John M. Miller out of an apartment in Brooklyn, New York. Drop him a line at etan@etan.org and he'll be delighted to tell you more.

As I have written in this book, one of the largest collections of material on Portuguese Timor is to be found inside Kevin Sherlock's walk-up apartment in Darwin. I found Kevin to be unfailingly helpful, and conversations on the old colonial days seem to animate him greatly. Kevin does not use email, so the best way to get in touch with him is via post: GPO Box 3223, Darwin, NT, 0801, Australia. Many of the people who read drafts of the book were bewitched by the story of Kevin and asked me what will happen to his remarkable collection once Kevin passes on. Not surprisingly, this conscientious man has that important detail organised: the collection will go to Charles Darwin University in the Northern Territory.

The Portuguese colonial period

Katherine G. Davison, *The Portuguese Colonisation of Timor: the final stage, 1850–1912* (Unpublished D. Phil thesis, Canberra: Australian National University 1994)

James J. Fox, *The Flow of Life: essays on Eastern Indonesia* (Cambridge: Harvard University Press 1980)

Han Hagerdal, *Conflict and Adaptation in Early Colonial Timor, 1600–1800* (Leiden: KITLV 2012)

Margaret King, *Eden to Paradise* (London: Hodder & Stoughton 1963)

Ricardo Roque, *Headhunting and Colonialism: anthropology and the circulation of human skulls in the Portuguese Empire, 1870–1930* (New York: Palgrave Macmillan 2010)

Osmar White, *Time Now, Time Before* (Melbourne: Heinemann 1967)

Civil war and short-lived independence

Jill Joliffe, *East Timor: nationalism and colonialism* (St Lucia: University of Queensland Press 1978)

Jill Joliffe, *Balibo* (Melbourne: Scribe 2009)

Tony Maniaty, *Shooting Balibo: blood and belonging in East Timor* (Melbourne: Penguin 2009)

Bill Nicol, *Timor: a nation reborn* (Jakarta: Equinox 2002)

The Indonesian occupation and its legacies

The Commission for Reception, Truth and Reconciliation in Timor-Leste, *Chega! Final Report of the Commission for Reception, Truth and Reconciliation in Timor-Leste* (Dili: 2005)

James Dunn, *Timor: a people betrayed* (Milton: Jacaranda 1983)

John Martinkus, *A Dirty Little War: an eyewitness account of East Timor's descent into hell* (Sydney: Random House 2001)

J. Modvig, J. Pagaduen-Lopez, J. Rodenburg, C.M.D. Salud, R.V. Cabigon, and C.I.A. Panelo, 'Torture and Trauma in Post-conflict East Timor', *The Lancet*, 18 November 2000.

Constancio Pinto and Matthew Jardine, *East Timor's Unfinished Struggle: inside the Timorese Resistance* (Brooklyn: South End Press 1999)

Geoffrey Robinson, *If You Leave Us Here, We Will Die: how genocide was stopped in East Timor* (Princeton: Princeton University Press 2010)

Post-independence

Irena Cristalis, *East Timor: a nation's bitter dawn* (London: Zed Books 2009)

UN Independent Special Commission of Inquiry for Timor-Leste (Geneva: United Nations 2006)

World Bank Independent Evaluation Group, *Timor-Leste Country Program Evaluation 2000–10* (Washington DC: 2010)

The reporting of the International Crisis Group on Timor-Leste, 2006–12

Language

Kerry Taylor-Leech, 'The Language Situation in Timor-Leste', *Current Issues in Language Planning*, (2009) 10, 1, pp. 1–68

Anacleto Ribeiro's (and others') contributions to the language debate is captured in http://www.scribd.com/doc/59602853/National-Languages-of-Timor-Leste-Conference-2010-Report

Oil and Gas

Paul Cleary, *Shakedown* (Sydney: Allen & Unwin 2007)

The painstakingly researched and consistently thoughtful pieces of *La'o Hamutuk* can be found at www.laohamutuk.org